Developing a
PRAYER-
CARE-
SHARE
Lifestyle

A Light-House
Devotional Guide

by
Alvin J. Vander Griend
Edith Bajema
John F. DeVries
David J. Deters

HOPE Ministries
Grand Rapids, Michigan

Cover and text design: Don Ellens

Developing a Prayer-Care-Share Lifestyle. Copyright © 1999, HOPE Ministries (a ministry of Mission India), P.O. Box 141312, Grand Rapids, MI 49514. 1-800-217-5200. All rights reserved. Except for brief excerpts for review or educational purposes, no part of this book may be reproduced in any manner whatever without written permission of the publisher.

10 9 8 7 6 5 4 3 2 1

Contents

Introduction

This devotional book is designed specifically for persons who are involved in a *Light-House of Prayer* ministry. A *Light-House* is a cluster of two or more believers banded together to pray for, care about, and share the blessings of Christ with those who live or work nearby. It can be located in any place where believers can pray for their neighbors—a home, a place of business, a work site, a college dorm, an apartment building, a prison—anywhere.

If you haven't yet started a *Light-House of Prayer* but want to, I suggest you begin by using the *Five Blessings* brochure from HOPE Ministries (1-800-217-5200 or www.hopeministries.org). This brochure describes how you can start simply by praying five blessings for five neighbors, five minutes a day, five days a week, for five weeks. You'll find it helpful!

Prayer, Care, and Share

A *Light-House* is a center of blessing. Through **prayer** you can have a remarkable influence in your neighborhood, workplace, or wherever you gather to pray. Your prayers can go where you can't go, and they can do what you can't do. That's because God, the Lord of heaven and earth, chooses to work through you as a praying believer in Christ. God wants you to join him in his great plan of salvation for this world, and he wants you to begin your work with him in prayer. In connection with your prayers God wants to open closed hearts, convey his healing, bring peace to persons who are troubled, and restore relationships. Isn't it amazing that God wants us to join him in this mysterious, wonderful work?

As you pray for your neighbors, God moves you to **care** more and more about them. And as you grow in your care for your neighbors, God leads you to show them the love of Christ in practical ways. Through God's love and leading, you help make Christ and Christianity attractive.

And just as praying leads to caring, caring leads to sharing. As you show your neighbors in various ways that you care for them, God gives you opportunities to **share** the good news of Jesus Christ with your neighbors. This means you will be working with God to bless your neighbors by giving them the opportunity to believe and be saved, to become part of the family of God. God will be working through you to build up his church and extend his kingdom!

The three sections of this book, each containing five weeks of five readings each, focus on the progression from *praying* for your neighbors, to *caring* about them, to *sharing* the good news of Jesus with them. Many practical ideas in the readings and ministry suggestions will give you a sense of how to do these things in a way that works for you—and for your neighbors.

How This Book Will Help You

This book will help you grow in prayer and learn how to pray effectively for the people around you. It will instruct you about prayer from key Scripture passages, stimulate growth through reflection and action questions, teach you to pray using the words of Scripture, and show you an easy way to remember basic life issues in prayer. You'll learn how to use the acronym *BLESS* as a way to remember five important ways to pray for neighbors: *B* stands for bodily needs, or physical needs; *L*, for labor or work concerns; *E*, for emotional needs; *S*, for social or relational areas of life; and the second *S*, for spiritual concerns.

This book will also help you become a more caring person for the people around you. It challenges you to take time with neighbors, reach out, break down walls, and turn words into actions. It will help you learn how to share the blessings of Christ more effectively—developing relationships, determining needs, and directing the gospel, the good news of Jesus.

At various points in the book you will find suggestions for ministry activity and faith-sharing. These suggestions offer ideas on practical ways to reach out to neighbors and to translate good intentions into actions. I urge you to take them seriously. Learning and spiritual growth happen best in a context of doing.

A Word About the Authors

This book is a combined effort, written by four authors.

The first section, "How Do I Pray for My Neighbors?" is reproduced from a booklet by the same name which I wrote in 1998.

The second section, "How Do I Care for My Neighbors?" is a compilation by three writers: Edith Bajema, a freelance writer living in Grand Rapids, Michigan; John F. DeVries, director of Mission India, the "parent" organization of HOPE Ministries; and myself. In that section the writer of each reading is identified by his or her initials: *EB, JDV,* and *AVG,* respectively.

The third section of the book, "How Do I Share with My Neighbors?" is written by David J. Deters, a pastor at Alger Park Christian Reformed Church in Grand Rapids.

I am deeply grateful to Edi, John, and David for their insightful contributions to this book.

Keep Growing, Keep Expanding

As you develop a "prayer-care-share lifestyle," keep trying to expand both the number of people you are praying *with* and the number of people you are praying *for.* Multiply your efforts by encouraging other Christians to start their own *Light-Houses of Prayer.*

Houses of Prayer Everywhere (HOPE) in Grand Rapids, Michigan, has many resources to help you understand and develop an effective *Light-House* ministry. Please contact us for a free brochure, a catalog, or an item you may wish to order or inquire about.

God has great expectations for you. He wants you to partner with him in evangelizing the world. You can play a significant role in his plan by praying for, caring about, and sharing the blessings of Christ with those who live or work near you. Be a light in the midst of a dark world; be a *Light-House of Prayer* for your God and Savior.

I pray that God will bless you as you embark on this adventure of praying for, caring for, and sharing Christ with your neighbors.

Prayerfully yours, in Christ,

Alvin J. Vander Griend
Director of HOPE Ministries

How Do I Pray for My Neighbors?

by Alvin J. Vander Griend

Contents

What's the Good of Prayer?

DAY 1

Friendship with God

You have made known to me the path of life;
you will fill me with joy in your presence,
with eternal pleasures at your right hand.

Psalm 16:11

Human beings are created to live in fellowship with God. We are meant to have and to enjoy relationship with God. Without this relationship we are like branches cut off from a tree, like lamps not plugged in.

Prayer is the way we get in touch with God and the way we keep in touch with him. I used to think of prayer as a spiritual exercise, a discipline that had to be worked at. Through the years, however, God has taught me to see it more and more as the talking part of a friendship. One of the early church fathers called it "keeping company with God." I like that!

Several years ago as I tried to define prayer, God led me through a series of steps. At first I thought of prayer simply as *talking with God.* Then the idea of relationship emerged, and I began to see that prayer is *the talking part of a relationship with God.* Months later my definition changed again, and I began to understand that prayer is *the talking part of a love relationship with God.* I thought I finally had it, but God added one more element. I came to see that *prayer is the talking part of the most important love relationship in my life.*

Sometimes people ask how much time they should try to spend in prayer each day. I used to suggest that 20 minutes of formal prayer a day was a minimum. I reinforced that by reminding them of the many things that need to be included in a prayer, and then I added that 20 minutes a day was only about 2 percent of our waking hours each day.

Now when people ask about the time they should spend in prayer, I simply tell them they should spend enough time to build a good relationship. And considering that the relationship we are talking about is life's most important love relationship, that means *plenty of time.*

What does God do for those who relate to him in love? The psalmist put it well when he said, "You will fill me with joy in your presence, with eternal pleasures at your right hand."

Are you spending enough time with God so that he has the opportunity to fill you with joy in his presence?

Reflect

- What can your prayer life tell you about your love relationship with God?
- What more could you do to deepen your friendship with God?

Prayer-Starters for Praying Psalm 16:11

Praise God for his love and for his readiness to have a love relationship with you.

Ask God to strengthen your prayer life and deepen your relationship with him.

Ask God to make known to you the path of life, to fill you with joy, and to give you eternal pleasures.

Thank God for his generosity in making these gifts available.

Pray a BLESSing on those who live or work near you:

Body (physical). Pray that the Father who sends "every good and perfect gift . . . from above" (James 1:17) will meet their needs.

Labor (work). Pray for diligence in work. "Lazy hands make a man poor, but diligent hands bring wealth" (Proverbs 10:4).

Emotional (inner life). Pray that they may have the Holy Spirit and his fruit. "The fruit of the Spirit is love, joy, peace, patience, kindness, goodness, faithfulness, gentleness and self-control" (Galatians 5:22-23).

Social (relational). Ask God to give them good friendships. "Pity the man who falls and has no one to help him up!" (Ecclesiastes 4:10).

Spiritual. Pray that they will "receive forgiveness of sins and a place among those who are sanctified by faith in [Christ]" (Acts 26:18).

Pray also for specific needs you are aware of.

DAY 2

Prayer Starts with God

The Spirit helps us in our weakness. We do not know what we ought to pray for, but the Spirit himself intercedes for us with groans that words cannot express. And he who searches our hearts knows the mind of the Spirit, because the Spirit intercedes for the saints in accord with God's will.

Romans 8:26-27

I want to share a radical thought. It has transformed my way of praying and my way of thinking about prayer.

For years I believed that my prayers started with me. I had to think them up. I had to get God's attention. Not surprisingly, with this frame of mind, prayer was often a chore.

I learned that I was wrong. Prayer doesn't start with us. *Prayer starts with God.* That's the radical idea that changed my prayer life. God is the initiator. He moves us to pray. He gives us prayer ideas. He holds out the promises we claim in prayer. When we pray, we are God's instruments.

God is at work in all our praying. He makes his will known to us so that we will ask for the very things he longs to give us. Out of love he burdens us to pray for others so that, in response to our intercession, he can pour out blessings on them.

And it's the Spirit, says Paul, that makes our prayer possible. We don't know what to pray, but we don't have to. The Spirit is there revealing God's will to us in the Scriptures and bringing God's prayer concerns to life within us. He is nudging us through circumstances and opening our eyes to the needs around us. He is searching our hearts and trying our ways so that he can bring us to true repentance. He is revealing the glory and the goodness of God so that our prayers will be filled with praise and thanks.

We can be confident that God will hear when we come to him. God answers every prayer that starts in heaven, every prayer born in our hearts by the Holy Spirit, every prayer based on a sure promise from his Word.

If prayer starts with God, then the first order of business as we learn to pray is to learn to listen to God's whispers, to tune our hearts to him, to respond to his promptings. Perhaps the first prayer of each day should be "Lord, teach me to pray. Help me to understand your purposes, to feel your burdens, to see what you see, to hear the groans you hear, so that my prayers may be pleasing to you and may accomplish your purposes."

How about starting right now: "Lord, teach me to pray today."

Reflect

- Is prayer a chore or a joy for you?
- What more could you do to be sure that you truly know God's will when you pray?

Prayer-Starters for Praying Romans 8:26-27

Praise the Lord as the prayer-initiating, prayer-hearing God.

Ask God to make prayer a joy in your life.

Thank God for the privilege of knowing his thoughts and praying them back to him.

Pray a BLESSing on those who live or work near you:

Body. Pray that the Father in heaven, who "causes his sun to rise on the evil and the good, and sends rain on the righteous and the unrighteous," will bless them (Matthew 5:45).

Labor. Pray that they may have employment and adequate compensation from it. "He who tends a fig tree will eat its fruit" (Proverbs 27:18).

Emotional. Pray that they will take their cares, hurts, and disappointments to the Lord. "Cast all your anxiety on him because he cares for you" (1 Peter 5:7).

Social. Pray for love, devotion, and sexual purity in marriages. "Marriage should be honored by all, and the marriage bed kept pure" (Hebrews 13:4).

Spiritual. Pray that they will call on the name of the Lord and be saved (Acts 2:21).

Pray for specific needs you are aware of.

Let the Holy Spirit nudge you on how to pray for your neighbors or work associates.

DAY 3

Celebrating God Through Prayer

I will extol the LORD at all times;
his praise will always be on my lips.
My soul will boast in the LORD;
let the afflicted hear and rejoice.
Glorify the LORD with me;
let us exalt his name together.

Psalm 34:1-3

Everyone loves a good celebration. And life gives us plenty of opportunities to celebrate. We celebrate Christmas, the new year, birthdays, anniversaries, graduations, victories, and more. But there is no better reason to celebrate than God.

To celebrate means "to honor or praise publicly." God deserves honor and praise more than anyone or anything else. The great Scottish preacher Alexander Whyte used to counsel his hearers to "think magnificently of God." People who think magnificently of God, calling to mind his greatness and goodness, cannot help but celebrate him and declare his praise.

We live in a society that delights to celebrate worth. We exalt athletic heroes, we gush over favorite movie stars, and we glory in our nations' victories. Not all of that is bad. But in the process of lifting up and extolling let's not forget the One who is the source of all good things.

To celebrate God means at least three things:

First, it means *recognizing God for who he is.* God's glory is his majestic splendor shining out so it can be seen and known. When we glorify God, we don't give him anything. We don't add luster to him. That's as impossible as it is to add splendor to a sunset by viewing it. But we can gaze in wonder at a sunset, and similarly we can behold in awe the beauty and glory of the Lord.

Second, it means *loving God for who he is.* This means laying aside our concerns, our demands, and our prayer lists to focus on God and to enjoy him. Nothing does more to quell pride, self-centeredness, and selfish desires than to focus beyond ourselves on God alone.

Third, celebrating God means *giving God the only thing we can offer him—* our loving, praising hearts. He already has everything else. He is totally self-sufficient and needs nothing from us. But God does ask us to give to him our hearts, our love, and our adoration. When we do, he is pleased and blessed.

16

Let's start today by thinking "magnificently of God." Everything else will follow.

Reflect

• How much do you enjoy God?
• What are some specific ways in which you can celebrate God today?

Prayer-Starters for Praying Psalm 34:1-3

Praise God by telling him five things you especially appreciate about him.

Ask God to help you see his majestic splendor and to truly enjoy him and love him.

Thank God for revealing his glory and for giving you reason to boast about him.

Pray a BLESSing on those who live or work near you:

Body. Pray that for all their needs they may look to God, who is prepared to "give them their food at the proper time" (Psalm 145:15).

Labor. Pray that they may keep their lives "free from the love of money and be content with what [they] have" (Hebrews 13:5).

Emotional. Pray that they may have "the unfading beauty of a gentle and quiet spirit, which is of great worth in God's sight" (1 Peter 3:4).

Social. Pray that they will "bear with each other and forgive whatever grievances [they] may have against one another" (Colossians 3:13).

Spiritual. Pray that they may confess Jesus as Lord, believe God raised him from the dead, and be saved (Romans 10:9).

Pray for specific needs of individuals on your prayer list.

Be open to impressions and burdens of the Holy Spirit, and pray as he leads you.

God Needs Our Prayers

"Choose some of our men and go out to fight the Amalekites. . . . I will stand on top of the hill with the staff of God in my hands." . . .
As long as Moses held up his hands, the Israelites were winning, but whenever he lowered his hands, the Amalekites were winning.

Exodus 17:9-11

God sometimes teaches us in surprising ways. When Israel faced a serious military threat, Joshua and the army went out to fight, but Moses went up on a hillside to pray. When his praying hands were up, Israel was winning. But when they were down, the enemy was winning.

Why, we may ask, would God allow his people to suffer defeat when there was no prayer? The answer is that God was teaching his people that he chooses to move in response to prayer and that he will not move without it.

Though he is almighty, all-wise, and fully able to work without us, God chooses to work through our prayers. He calls us into a working partnership. Without us, he won't work.

When God first taught me this important principle of prayer, it had a simple but pointed application for me. It was as if God said, "Alvin, when your children go to school each morning, they are heading into battle. If you as a parent keep your hands uplifted, they will be winning. But, if your praying hands come down, they will be losing." I have never forgotten that lesson.

Since that time I have come to see that as church leaders and faithful Christians "lift up holy hands in prayer" (1 Timothy 2:8), the church grows strong and is able to break down the gates of hell. When believers in neighborhoods and workplaces lift up praying hands over those around them, the powers of darkness are pushed back.

The most common testimony of *Light-House of Prayer* members as they pray over neighborhoods is that of transformation. They speak of drug houses closing, crime rates falling, marriages being restored, families coming back together, and people being converted. What's happening as God's people pray over their neighborhoods is the same thing that happened as Moses prayed over the battlefield. The forces of evil go into retreat.

What we need most for solving the problems in our society is not more money, more education, more ideas, books, or strategies. Our prime need is hands lifted up in prayer. "We can accomplish far more by our prayers than by our work. Prayer . . . can do anything God can do! When we pray, God works" (*The Kneeling Christian*). Where are your hands right now?

Reflect

- Where in God's kingdom are people winning against the powers of darkness because of your prayers?
- What kinds of things do you think God might want to do on your street or at your workplace in response to your prayers?

Prayer-Starters for Praying Exodus 17:9-11

Praise God for the wisdom of his plan to govern the world through the prayers of his people.

Ask God to help you understand why your prayers are so important to him.

Thank God for honoring you by choosing to act in response to your prayers.

Commit yourself to pray faithfully for neighbors or work associates so that God may work in response to your prayers.

Pray a blessing on your neighbors, using the pattern of the Lord's Prayer:

Think of each household you are praying for, and ask that God will hallow his name in each place, establish his kingdom and destroy the works of the powers of darkness, and help each person involved to know and do God's will as the angels in heaven do.

Pray that each person or household will have their daily needs met, will repent and find forgiveness of sins, and will be kept from temptation and the devil's snares.

Thank God that he is willing and able to answer this prayer, because his is "the kingdom and the power and the glory forever."

DAY 5

Your Welcome to the Throne

Let us then approach the throne of grace with confidence, so that we may receive mercy and find grace to help us in our time of need.
Hebrews 4:16

Access to the throne of God is the foundation of all prayer. All "pray-ers" must approach the throne. Every true believer is welcome there.

Access to God's throne is an amazing privilege. The One we approach is the sovereign, all-powerful, holy Ruler of the universe. What a privilege to be welcomed into his presence!

God's throne, we are reminded, is a throne of grace, not a throne of judgment. This means that if we have come into his presence through the blood of Christ, we are acceptable to him. God doesn't scrutinize us to screen out unworthiness. He extends a hand of welcome.

We are invited to approach with complete confidence. We won't run into a closed door. We won't have to beg or grovel to get in. God is expecting us. He is glad we have come.

Sometimes when I pray, I like to imagine myself right there in the throne room of heaven. In my mind's eye I see the One upon the throne high and lifted up. His glory fills the room. I see angels all around. It's enough to overpower me with dread, except for one thing: God recognizes me. He knows my name. He looks at me, smiles, and extends a hand of welcome. "Tell me why you have come," he says.

This wonderful welcome is not extended to us because we are so good and worthy in ourselves. The truth is, we deserve to be barred from his presence because of our sins. But Christ has dealt with our sins and made us acceptable to God. We have been adopted as sons and daughters. We have a place in the royal family.

We can come to the throne with our own concerns. We can also come, as intercessors, with the needs of our families, friends, and neighbors on our hearts.

Intercessors in *Light-Houses of Prayer* regularly talk to God on behalf of their neighbors. One *Light-House* member reported that after she and others had prayed for their neighbors for about a year, neighbors became more friendly, people stopped abusing drugs, two unemployed women found jobs, a father stopped drinking, a woman was miraculously cured, a person was delivered from an evil spirit, several persons came to know Christ, and a Bible study began. Wow! What was happening in the throne room had a transforming effect on earth.

That's something of what God has in mind by extending his welcome to us. He wants to change us, and he wants to change our world.

Reflect
- Why is it possible for believers to approach the throne of God with confidence?
- How much confidence do you have when you pray?
- What are some ways in which you could increase your confidence?

Prayer-Starters for Praying Hebrews 4:16
Praise God for making his grace and mercy available for the asking.

Ask God for the mercy and grace he generously offers to you.

Ask God for the confidence you need so that you can pray effectively for yourself and others.

Thank God for his welcome.

Pray, as guided by the Spirit, for those who live or work near you:
Discern God's guidance as you pray for your friends, neighbors, or work associates by seeking the answers to questions like these:

What strongholds may be holding them in bondage to the evil one?

What false concepts of God may be keeping them from turning to him?

What sins are they unwilling to relinquish?

What misunderstandings are causing them to hold back?

Let your prayers be directed by what you sense and by the promptings of the Holy Spirit.

The Requirements of Prayer

DAY 1

The Necessity of a Clean Heart

If I had cherished sin in my heart,
*   the LORD would not have listened;*
but God has surely listened
*   and heard my voice in prayer.*

Psalm 66:18-19

Sin hinders prayer. A person may pray and pray without receiving an answer, and then conclude that the problem is in God. In reality the problem may be in the person's heart. David understood that if he cherished sin in his heart, the Lord would not hear him.

One of the worst things about sin is that it obstructs prayer. We are shut out from God when we cherish sin because he is holy and cannot tolerate sin in his presence.

When sin blocks prayer, the real problem is not that we have sinned but that, having sinned, we have not repented. It is only unconfessed sin, cherished in our hearts, that inhibits our prayers. Forgiven sin does not hinder prayer. Forgiven sinners are welcome in God's presence.

Always eager to have us come into his presence, God has provided a way for sin to be removed through Jesus' blood so that we can come and not be hindered. John says, "If we confess our sins, he is faithful and just and will forgive us our sins and purify us from all unrighteousness" (1 John 1:9). When it's forgiven, our sin is gone, and it no longer impedes.

The first requirement of prayer, then, is to confess anything in your heart that is not of God. When your sin is forgiven, you can be confident that God will hear and answer your prayers.

Don't be afraid to take inventory and to deal with what you find. Recently when I was confronted with a list of twenty sin-identifying Scripture texts, I at first thought, "My heart is clean before God. I don't have anything to confess." But I went through the list anyway, and to my amazement I found five areas of sin that needed to be dealt with. So I clearly identified what was offensive to God, confessed those things, and claimed God's forgiving grace. Through that I again discovered complete freedom in prayer. We can't have the privilege of prayer without purity of heart.

Not only does sin hinder prayer; prayer hinders sin. The two are always opposed. The more careless we are about sin, the less we will pray. The more we pray, the less careless we will be about sin. Both sin and prayer are powerful forces. Which one is moving you?

Reflect

- Is there any area of your life about which you are uneasy before God? Risk taking a closer look at it. You may find a "cherished" sin.
- Can you say to yourself with confidence what David said: "God has surely listened and heard my voice in prayer"?

Prayer-Starters for Praying Psalm 66:18-19

Praise God that "he is faithful and just and will forgive us our sins" (1 John 1:9).

Ask God to search your heart and life and reveal to you any sin that you may need to deal with. Then confess whatever he finds.

Thank God for forgiving your sin and purifying you from all unrighteousness so that you can go confidently into his presence.

Pray a BLESSing on those who live or work near you:

Body (physical). Pray that God will meet their needs "according to his glorious riches in Christ Jesus" (Philippians 4:19).

Labor (work). Pray that they may live quiet lives, mind their own business, and work with their hands so that they may win the respect of others and not be dependent on anyone (1 Thessalonians 4:11-12).

Emotional (inner life). Pray for those who are depressed, that they may have peace of heart and mind and may put their hope in God (Psalm 42:5).

Social (relational). Pray that they may have good friends who will stick by them at all times and family members who will stand by them in adversity (Proverbs 17:17).

Spiritual. Pray that the kindness of God will lead them to repentance (Romans 2:4).

Pray for specific needs of individuals and families on your prayer list.

DAY 2

The Faith That Receives

"Have faith in God," Jesus answered. . . . "Therefore I tell you, whatever you ask for in prayer, believe that you have received it, and it will be yours."

Mark 11:22-24

Faith is a second requirement of true prayer. Prayers without faith are incomplete. Millions of prayers have been prayed with no faith and have thus failed in their intent. They were not true prayer.

The astounding promise Jesus makes in Mark 11:24 seems to offer too much. How can God offer to do "whatever [we] ask for in prayer"? And why have so many believers asked, trusting him, and not received?

The difficulty we have with this passage is really a difficulty in understanding faith. We tend to think of faith as a personal possession that exists wholly within us. We figure that if we have enough faith, we get what we ask for—and if we don't, we won't get it.

But faith is not simply a possession. It's an aspect of relationship. It's not something we own like an idea or a feeling. Faith always involves another person. It trusts the other person to think and act in a certain way. For example, throughout all the years my parents were alive, I knew they would welcome me anytime I came home. I knew they loved me. I trusted that they cared for me and were willing to help me anytime. In other words, I had faith in them. This faith was based on what I knew about them. Faith in God is like that. It's a conviction about who he is, what he is like, and how he will always act.

Praying in faith is not an inner conviction that God will act according to our desires if only we believe hard enough. It's believing that God will always respond to our prayers in accord with his nature, his purposes, and his promises.

God does not want us simply to toss requests at him, hoping that some of them will be answered. He wants us to ask, knowing he is there, claiming what he promises, trusting that he will act in line with his nature and that his purposes will be achieved. That's praying in faith.

When you ask a person for something in good faith, you don't ask for something the person would not be willing to give. I could never, for example, ask my parents to give me more than my share of their inheritance. I knew them too well to ask that. Similarly, if you truly know God, you will only ask for what is in accord with his will and not for anything that is purely selfish.

If you want to grow strong in prayer, grow strong in faith. If you want to grow strong in faith, get to know God better. If you want to get to know God better, spend time with him, reading his Word and listening to his Spirit.

Reflect
- Why do you think God has made faith such an indispensable condition of prayer?
- What kinds of things can you do to increase your faith?

Prayer-Starters for Praying Mark 11:22-24
Praise God for being trustworthy.

Ask God to increase your faith so that you can pray more powerfully.

Thank God for his willingness to hear and answer the prayers you bring to him in faith.

Pray a BLESSing on those who live or work near you:
Body. Pray that God will give them the discipline to eat healthfully, to exercise as needed, and to maintain habits that will enhance their health.

Labor. Pray that whatever their hands find to do, they may do it with all their might (Ecclesiastes 9:10).

Emotional. Isaiah said, "The fruit of righteousness will be peace; the effect of righteousness will be quietness and confidence forever" (Isaiah 32:17). Pray that they may be righteous and may experience the fruits of peace, quietness, and confidence.

Social. Give thanks for your neighbors. Pray that God will help them see the qualities of, and give thanks for, the people they relate to (Philippians 1:3).

Spiritual. Pray that they may have faith to believe that God exists "and that he rewards those who earnestly seek him" (Hebrews 11:6).

Pray for the needs of those who live or work near you, as prompted by the Holy Spirit. Trust that God is moving in response to your prayers.

DAY 3

The Life That Can Pray

We have confidence before God and receive from him anything we ask, because we obey his commands and do what pleases him.

1 John 3:21-22

Obedience is fundamental to effective prayer. Only those who obey God have the right to go into his presence with requests.

God delights in the prayers of his obedient children. When we want what God wants and live the way he likes, then we will tend to pray prayers that God will answer in the way we expect. And God, in answering our prayers, is supporting what he approves. Were he to answer the prayers of the disobedient, he would be aiding and abetting what he does not approve. That would not be like God.

To put it in other words, if we expect God to do for us what we ask, we should be prepared to do for him what he asks. If we listen to his words of command, God will listen to our words of request.

This principle also explains much of the weakness of prayer. Lack of power, lack of perseverance, and lack of confidence in prayer all stem from some lack in the Christian life. Often when prayer fails and we receive no answers, we assume the problem is in God, while in reality the problem really is in us.

The obedience God expects of us is not beyond our reach. God, who is committed to hearing the prayers of his obedient children, also gives enabling grace so that we will be able to live obediently. Touched by his grace and indwelt by his Spirit, we have both the desire and strength to do his will.

If you want to become powerful in prayer, spend time with the Lord and spend much time in the Word. That's where you will find the will of God clearly stated. Let "the word of Christ dwell in you richly" and control what you do and say (Colossians 3:16). Jesus reminds us that if we remain in him, and his words remain in us, we may ask whatever we wish and it will be given us (John 15:7).

Or, to put it more simply, let me ask, Do you want to have confidence when you pray and receive from God what you ask for? Commit yourself to living a life of obedience. By God's grace and with his spirit living in you, you can do it! That's the bottom line.

Reflect

- What difference will confidence make in your prayer life?
- What kinds of things will confident "pray-ers" ask for?
- What kinds of things do you think God is eager to give to those who obey his commands?

Prayer-Starters for Praying 1 John 3:21-22

Praise God for his generous, giving nature.

Confess any failure to keep God's commands or to do what pleases him.

Ask God for the desires of your obedient heart.

Thank God for this amazing promise to answer prayer.

Pray for the persons around you, using ideas from Paul's prayer in Colossians 1:9-12:

Pray that they may be full of the knowledge of God's will.

Pray that they may learn to live in a way that is worthy of the Lord and pleasing to him.

Pray that they may bear fruit for God in all their works.

Pray that they may grow in their knowledge of God.

Pray that they may be strengthened by the Holy Spirit to do good and resist evil.

Pray that they will be able to joyfully give thanks to the Father.

DAY 4

Praying in Jesus' Name

"Until now you have not asked for anything in my name. Ask and you will receive, and your joy will be complete."

John 16:24

By offering to let us pray in his name, Jesus is offering an amazingly great privilege. It's as if he is giving us blank checks to be drawn on his account, knowing we will use them for his honor and his advantage.

Jesus is demonstrating great trust in us. He is trusting that his honor and his interests are safe in our hands. Consider what it would mean to place your estate in the hands of another person: your credit cards, your home, your investments, your automobiles, your responsibilities, everything. You'd pick that person very carefully, wouldn't you? You'd really be giving that person control over your life and your future.

That's essentially what Jesus did when he authorized us to use his name in prayer. He gave us authority over his accounts. He asked us to exercise control over his estate—the kingdom of God.

We exercise our authority by prayer. By prayer we ask the Father for all that we need to do the job. By prayer we ask God to deal with demonic forces contrary to his will. By prayer we direct God's grace and power to strategic locations where it is needed.

Three phrases in particular help us understand what it means to pray in Jesus' name. First, we are *authorized to be Christ's representatives*. When we come to the Father in Jesus' name, we come as those who are authorized to act in his place. We "re-present" him. When we stand before the throne, the Father recognizes us as persons who stand in the place of his Son. That makes us acceptable.

Second, we come to God *on the basis of Christ's merit*. You and I have no claim on God, but Christ does. He merited the Father's favor by his perfect life and sacrifice. When we come in Jesus' name, we are identified with him. We come on the ground of his claim on the Father. Our access depends solely on what Jesus has done.

Try to imagine yourself coming to the Father on your own, apart from Christ. You are unauthorized to come, because you have no claim on God's favor. In fact, you have a huge debt with God because of your sins and you can expect nothing but his blazing wrath. That's the opposite of coming in the name of Jesus.

Third, we come asking *in accord with Christ's will*. We have the mind of Christ in us, so what we ask is what he would ask. He is asking us to ask for him. We are able to ask what he would ask because our wills are in sync with his will.

The Father so loves the Son that when we introduce the Son's name in prayer, we have his ear, we have secured his willingness, we have touched his heart.

Reflect

- Think about the part of Christ's kingdom you have been given responsibility for. What's needed there to advance the kingdom?
- What can you do to learn how to pray more consciously in Jesus' name?

Prayer-Starters for Praying John 16:24

Praise God for his gracious provision of his Son, Jesus Christ, as the One through whom you are able to approach the throne and receive a hearing from God.

Confess any selfish praying that has not truly represented the mind of Christ and has not been in accord with his will.

Ask for anything you need in order to accomplish God's will in your life and in your world.

Pray an expanded version of the Lord's Prayer (Matthew 6:9-13) for those who live or work near you:

God's Concerns. Pray that they may know the Father who is in heaven, that their lives will glorify God, that his kingdom will be established in their homes and workplaces, and that they will desire to do his will as do the angels in heaven.

Human Concerns. Pray that God will provide for their daily needs, forgive their sins, keep them from falling into temptation, and protect them from the devil's schemes.

DAY 5

Praying with Persistence

Jesus told his disciples a parable to show them that they should always pray and not give up.

Luke 18:1 (also read vv. 2-8)

Prayer is not always easy. Sometimes it requires serious persistence in the face of great difficulty and delayed answers. God wants us to rise above weakness and become mighty in prayer. The parable of the persistent widow in Luke 18:2-8 strikingly illustrates this principle.

To pray persistently is to press our requests upon God with urgency and perseverance. It means praying boldly and with determination until the answer comes.

When God delays his answers to prayer, it is always with good reason. Sometimes he does it to deepen our faith and develop our character. Sometimes he does it to test our faith and put it on display. Sometimes he is simply operating according to a divine timetable that seems slow to us. When answers are slow in coming, it's important to simply keep trusting God.

God has called us to persistent prayer so that his will may be done on earth and his name glorified. We may never use prayer for selfish reasons. Prayer is the means by which God accomplishes his purposes and defeats Satan. Through prayer we are involved with him in a grand enterprise. And the going is not always easy.

George Mueller is a good example of persistence in prayer. He prayed daily for five unsaved friends. One of them came to Christ after five years; two more were converted after fifteen years. The fourth was saved after thirty-five years of prayer, and the fifth became a child of God just after Mueller's death.

Passion in prayer is usually tied closely to perseverance in prayer. Passion does not spring simply from human emotion or earnestness of soul. It's an urgency derived from God who, through his Spirit within us, gives us both the content and the passion of our prayers.

Weak and feeble praying does not have the power to overcome difficulties and gain the victory. E. M. Bounds asserted, "Heaven pays little attention to casual requests. God is not moved by feeble desires, listless prayers, and spiritual laziness."

There is great need today for powerful, persistent prayer. Much is accomplished through persistent prayer that is not accomplished by timid, halting prayers. God has much to accomplish through you—in your world, in your church, in your family, and in your neighborhood. I urge you to partner with God through passionate, persistent prayer.

Reflect

- Which comes closer to describing your intercessory prayer life: bold, passionate, and persevering or casual, weak, and fainthearted?
- What things in your life might God want you to pray about persistently?

Prayer-Starters for Praying Luke 18:1-8

Praise God, who hears prayer and "brings about justice for his chosen ones, who cry to him day and night" (Luke 18:7).

Confess whatever casualness, weakness, feebleness, superficiality, laxity, faintheartedness, or impatience you may discover as you examine your prayer life.

Ask the Holy Spirit for boldness, power, devotion, persistence, and a sense of urgency in your prayer life.

Thank God for the privilege of partnering with him through prayer in accomplishing his will on earth.

Pray a BLESSing on those who live or work near you:

Body. Pray that they will find God to be good and "a refuge in times of trouble" (Nahum 1:7).

Labor. Pray that those with an inclination toward idleness may "settle down and earn the bread they eat" (2 Thessalonians 3:12).

Emotional. Pray that in times of trouble they will pray to God and will discover the peace of God that passes all understanding in Jesus Christ (Philippians 4:7).

Social. Pray that children will obey and honor their parents and that parents will train and instruct their children in the things of the Lord (Ephesians 6:1-4).

Spiritual. Pray that they will "seek the Lord while he may be found; call on him while he is near," and be freely pardoned (Isaiah 55:6-7).

Prayerwalk your neighborhood so that you can pray "on-site with insight."

Prayerwalking

Now that you have prayed for your neighbors for *two weeks*, why not try a brief prayerwalk past the homes or workplaces of those you are praying for?

Prayerwalking is putting feet to our prayers—"praying on-site with insight." Just walk through your neighborhood or place of business and talk to God about things you see, hear, or feel.

Guidelines for Prayerwalking

- Pray for the Spirit's help before you go. Ask God to help you see things through his eyes.

- Go alone or with another member of your *Light-House of Prayer*. Pray aloud as you pass each home or work station, if you can do so without being overheard by those you are praying for.

- Pray with your eyes open. Observe realities, needs, and people. Talk to God about these.

- Ask God to release his power and grace in their lives. Pray especially for their salvation.

- Never be obvious, just persistent.

The Value of Prayerwalking

- On-site, we pray with greater insight.

- Drawing nearer, our prayers become clearer.

- Being present, we are better able to pray the presence of Christ into our neighborhood.

Practical Helps for Prayerwalking

Try one of the following approaches as you start prayerwalking.

1. **Pray the kind of BLESSing you have learned to pray** in the previous devotional readings. You'll find yourself putting new and more specific content into the BLESS outline when you are actually on-scene.

2. **Pray an expanded version of the Lord's Prayer.** This prayer signals the major things God wants to have in your neighborhood—his name hallowed, his kingdom established, and his will done. It also reveals the things he is willing to provide—bread, forgiveness, and spiritual protection.

3. Pray as you are prompted by visible neighborhood cues.

→ Seeing your neighbors' earthly *home* may prompt you to pray that they will have a heavenly home.

→ A *door* may remind you that Jesus Christ knocks at their door seeking to gain entry.

→ *Windows* may prod you to pray for openings in their lives to the light of the Son.

→ *Flowers* may move you to pray that they be blessed with inner beauty and fragrance.

→ The presence of *children* may stimulate a prayer that these little ones may come to Jesus and not be hindered (Matthew 19:14).

→ Observing *trees* in the yard may encourage you to pray that your neighbors will be fruit-bearing branches of Christ, the true vine (John 15:1-8).

Claiming God's Riches

DAY 1

Asking for Ourselves

Let us then approach the throne of grace with confidence, so that we may receive mercy and find grace to help us in our time of need.
                              Hebrews 4:16 (also read vv. 14-15)

"Whether we like it or not," said Charles H. Spurgeon, "asking is the rule of the kingdom." God delights in our asking because we are his children. His Father-heart leaps for joy when we come asking.

Petition is asking God for our personal needs. I want to emphasize here that it's okay to request God's blessings for ourselves. Some people think petition (asking for ourselves) is a more primitive form of prayer, reflecting a still-somewhat-selfish spirituality, while prayers of praise, thanksgiving, and inter-cession reflect a higher kind of spirituality.

That's unbiblical thinking. We are forever dependent on God, so we need constantly to be asking for his blessing on us. God has much to give, and we have great need. Petitionary prayer connects our needs to God's generosity. In Hebrews 4:16 we are urged to approach God's throne of grace with confidence to receive what we need from him.

In an obscure Old Testament passage in the midst of a long list of names, one person is singled out, and his prayer patterns are lifted up as an example (1 Chronicles 4:9-10). His name is Jabez. Here's what the Bible says about him: "Jabez cried out to the God of Israel, 'Oh, that you would bless me and enlarge my territory! Let your hand be with me, and keep me from harm so that I will be free from pain.' And God granted his request." Jabez prayed a prayer of petition. He asked a personal blessing from God, and it was granted. God still works this way in our lives today. He hasn't changed the "rule of asking."

God invites us to come with confidence in the awareness that Jesus Christ has opened the way to God's Father-heart for our sake.

God invites us to come with a consciousness of our sin, asking for mercy. He invites us to come with a consciousness of our needs, asking for grace to help. Jesus stands ready to meet us, no matter what our need may be.

It's an insult to God not to come asking. Saint Theresa of Avila once declared, "You pay God a compliment by asking great things of him."

What are you going to ask?

Reflect

- Have you ever felt complimented by being asked for help? Why might asking be a way to compliment God? Why might God be insulted if we don't ask?
- Why do you suppose that God, knowing us better than we know ourselves, has invited us to come asking?

Prayer-Starters for Praying Hebrews 4:16

Praise Jesus Christ, our heavenly High Priest, who has entered into the heavenly throne room for us, who is also able to sympathize fully with us.

If you have failed to regularly approach the throne of grace to ask for mercy and grace, *confess* this as an insult to God and a failure to recognize the true nature of your dependence on him.

Thank God for his readiness to forgive and to help you in time of need.

Approach God with confidence and ask for the mercy he has promised and for the grace to help you with any specific need.

Pray a BLESSing on those who live or work near you:

Body. Pray that they may seek the kingdom of God first and receive all other blessings they need as well (Matthew 6:33).

Labor. Pray that they will be kept from the love of money and will be content with what they have (Hebrews 13:5).

Emotional. The Word of God says, "Whoever listens to me will live in safety and be at ease, without fear of harm" (Proverbs 1:33). Pray that your neighbors will listen to God and receive his promised blessings.

Social. Pray that they may have many good friends who will stick "closer than a brother" (Proverbs 18:24).

Spiritual. Pray that people's hearts will be open to believe (Acts 16:14).

DAY 2

Asking for Good Things

"Which of you, if his son asks for bread, will give him a stone? Or if he asks for a fish, will give him a snake? If you, then, though you are evil, know how to give good gifts to your children, how much more will your Father in heaven give good gifts to those who ask him!"

Matthew 7:9-11

As a father, I have always wanted good things for our four children. I have deeply desired that they have firm faith, wholesome morals, excellent educational opportunities, fine friends, good jobs, strong marriages, lovely children, and stable lives. I have hoped and prayed that their lives may be full of love, joy, and peace. I have wanted all this despite the fact that, as an earthly father, I don't hold a candle to the heavenly Father.

Jesus makes clear that our heavenly Father, who is perfect in his love and unlimited in power, wants good things for us, his children. And he assures us that the Father is willing to give good gifts to his children, much more willing than any earthly father or mother.

There's just one hitch. In order to receive the good things the Father wants for them, his children have to ask. Not to ask is not to receive. That's what some spiritually deprived believers found out the hard way. James said to them, "You do not have, because you do not ask God" (James 4:2).

The "good things" Jesus has in mind are the spiritual blessings of grace, wisdom, joy, peace, power, holiness, and so on. These are things in accord with God's will. We can ask the Father for them with absolute assurance that he will give them to us. It's what he has promised.

What an amazing promise! Getting hold of this promise revolutionized my spiritual life. I searched the Scriptures for the good things God wanted for me. I asked for them. And, true to his promise, God began to give them—not in huge once-for-all doses, but little by little. Every time I began to ask for some new "good thing," if I watched closely, I began to see God working this good thing into my life.

God is eager to give. He's on the lookout for children who will take him at his word and ask in faith. As one Old Testament prophet put it: "The eyes of the LORD range throughout the earth to strengthen those whose hearts are fully committed to him" (2 Chronicles 16:9).

He's probably looking at you right now and wondering what good things you are going to ask him for. I have a feeling he'll be disappointed if you don't go for the max and ask him for all sorts of really good things—things that he is really eager to give you—right now.

Reflect
- What good things would you give to your family members or friends if you could?
- What do you prize most highly among God's good gifts?
- Why is it important to God that we ask?

Prayer-Starters for Praying Matthew 7:9-11

Praise the Father, who in his power and love is able and willing to give "good things" to those who ask.

Confess any attempt to fill your life with worldly things instead of the good things the Father wants to give you.

Ask for all the spiritually good things you can think of.

Thank God in advance for what he will send in response to your prayer.

Pray for those who live or work near you, using ideas from Psalm 121:

Pray that the Lord who has made heaven and earth will be moved to help them.

Pray that the Lord will not let them slip from their spiritual walk with him.

Pray that the Lord will watch over them with sleepless vigilance.

Pray that he will keep them from all harm.

Pray that he will watch over their lives.

Pray that he will watch over their coming and going, both now and eternally.

Pray that God will open doors of opportunity for you to connect with your neighbors and work associates, and that God will enable you to share with them in meaningful ways.

DAY 3

Getting What We Ask For

This is the confidence we have in approaching God: that if we ask any-thing according to his will, he hears us. And if we know that he hears us—whatever we ask—we know that we have what we asked of him.
1 John 5:14-15

Imagine what it would be like to approach God in prayer and receive from him anything and everything we asked for. I'm sure we would do a lot of ask-ing if that were the case. Once the pattern of asking and receiving became established, we'd be bold to go back and ask for more.

Well, God doesn't promise to give us anything and everything we ask for. But he does make an astonishing promise to "pray-ers" that is even better. He promises to give us whatever we ask that is "according to his will."

To ask for what is according to God's will is to ask for the very things he wants for us. These are the things he knows we need, the things that are truly good for us, the riches of his grace that he wants us to have.

How do we know what is according to God's will? We look in the Bible. There God tells us what he most wants for us.

When I first understood this principle and wanted to pray in accord with God's will, the Holy Spirit took me to Romans 8:29 and reminded me that God wanted me "to be conformed to the likeness of his Son." Then I did a very sim-ple thing. I said, "God, please conform me to the image of your Son." That was the first prayer I consciously prayed in accord with God's will. God heard me and began in me the process that answered that prayer. He's still working at it today.

After that, I found many things to ask for that were in accord with God's will for me. I asked for wisdom, faith, virtue, love, joy, godliness, prayerful-ness, Spirit-filledness, and much more. I know God heard those prayers. I began to see the difference it made in me. What I usually observed was a defi-nite but gradual change in the right direction.

If you want to grow spiritually and to claim the riches God has for you, sim-ply ask for those things in accord with God's will. He will hear, and you will receive what you ask of him. God has promised to give what you ask for in accord with his will.

And if what you ask for happens to be outside of his will and you don't receive it, thank God! What's outside of his will isn't good for you anyway.

Reflect

- Think about the patterns you practice in prayer. Are you used to approaching God with confidence that he will hear and respond, or do you pray just hoping something will happen?
- What things can you ask God for right now that you know are in his will for you?

Prayer-Starters for Praying 1 John 5:14-15

Praise God for the wisdom by which he knows what is best for you, and for the power to do what he promises.

Confess if you find that because of weakness in your prayers you have failed to claim the riches God has promised you.

Ask God for spiritual riches that you know are "according to his will" for your life.

Thank God for what he will give even before you actually receive it. If you can honestly do this, it's a sure sign that you really trust God to deliver on his promise.

Pray a BLESSing on those who live or work near you:

Body. Pray that God will cover them "with his feathers," give them refuge under his wings, and be to them a "shield and rampart" (Psalm 91:4).

Labor. Pray that they will make good use of the opportunities God has given them and not sleep "during harvest" (Proverbs 10:5).

Emotional. Pray that they may "turn from evil and do good; seek peace and pursue it" (Psalm 34:14).

Social. Pray that family members and friends will be a source of joy and blessing to each other and may experience together the blessing of the Lord.

Spiritual. Pray that the unsaved persons you name before God may seek him, reach out to him, and find him, since "he is not far from each one of us" (Acts 17:27).

DAY 4

The Cure for Anxiety

Do not be anxious about anything, but in everything, by prayer and petition, with thanksgiving, present your requests to God. And the peace of God, which transcends all understanding, will guard your hearts and your minds in Christ Jesus.

Philippians 4:6-7

It happens regularly nowadays. A beeper goes off in a room full of people. In response to the beeper, someone gets up, leaves the room, and makes a phone call. Something is in need of immediate attention. The phone call takes care of it.

Life is full of things that need immediate attention. Problems, frustrations, and distresses can produce anxiety and rob us of peace. God doesn't want this to happen, so he has provided a way that we can get in touch with him immediately when anxiety attacks.

Anxiety is like a beeper system alerting us that it's time to talk to God about a situation that worries us. When anxiety threatens, God invites us to come to him in prayer and promises that he will restore peace in our lives.

Or the anxiety may be sent by God, like a referee whistling the game of our lives to a temporary halt because the rules have been broken. Sin may be the cause of the anxiety—in which case peace is restored when we repent and God forgives.

We are welcome to come to God with anything, large or small. Nothing is too great for his power; nothing is too small for him to deal with. If it is a concern to you, it is a concern to God.

We're encouraged to come "with thanksgiving." Thanksgiving arises from remembering who God is and what he does for us. Remember that God is love and that nothing can separate us from his love (1 John 4:16; Romans 8:38-39). Remember that his goodness and mercy will follow you all the days of your life (Psalm 23:6), and you will always be thankful.

The result of prayer is peace—"the peace of God, which transcends all understanding"—a peace that is beyond the ability of humans to contrive or produce.

God not only works out the situations we place in his hands for our good (Romans 8:28); he also works in us to "guard our hearts and minds in Christ Jesus" (Philippians 4:7).

Is God getting your attention through anxiety? Get in touch with him immediately. Don't delay! He'll be glad to have you come. He's invited you. He has a wonderful peace to give you.

Reflect

- Think about how you have handled anxiety in the past. Is there some way you can improve your way of handling anxiety based on this Scripture passage?
- What signs would you look for to confirm that you have handled anxiety in a God-pleasing way?

Prayer-Starters for Praying Philippians 4:6-7

Praise God, the hearer of prayer, the peace giver, the one who guards your heart and mind in Jesus Christ.

Ask God to forgive you for any times you may have handled anxiety improperly.

Thank God for the peace he gives in the midst of troubling situations.

Ask God to give you peace and to guard your heart and mind.

Pray a BLESSing on your neighbors or work associates:

Body. Pray that God may be a "refuge and strength, an ever-present help in trouble"(Psalm 46:1).

Labor. Give prayer support to them in their work and their studies and pray that each may be diligent in pursuit of their God-given tasks.

Emotional. Pray that they will "not be anxious in anything, but in everything, by prayer and petition, with thanksgiving, [will] present [their] requests to God" (Philippians 4:6).

Social. Pray for couples undergoing marital strife. Ask that God will rekindle a flame of love between husband and wife.

Spiritual. Pray that unsaved persons hearing the Word will accept it as truly the Word of God (1 Thessalonians 2:13).

DAY 5

When God Says "No"

There was given me a thorn in my flesh, a messenger of Satan, to torment me. Three times I pleaded with the Lord to take it away from me. But he said to me, "My grace is sufficient for you, for my power is made perfect in weakness."

2 Corinthians 12:7-9

Someone has suggested that God answers prayer in the following five ways:
- *"Yes! I thought you would never ask."*
- *"Yes! But not yet."*
- *"No! I love you too much."*
- *"Yes! But different from your thoughts."*
- *"Yes! But more than you ever hoped or dreamed."*

Let's look briefly at each one of these.

"Yes! I thought you would never ask." Here's a reminder that God has so many good things to give us that he can hardly wait till we ask for them. When we finally ask, he is quick to answer.

"Yes! But not yet." When God asks us to wait, it may seem like a "no" answer. But it's really a delayed "yes." When God delays an answer to prayer, it's always for a good reason. He may be teaching us to depend wholly on him, preparing us to receive the answer when it comes, or simply refining our prayers.

"No! I love you too much." God's wisdom is higher than our wisdom. When what we ask is not good for us, God graciously answers "no." He loves us too much to fulfill our wishes against his better judgment.

"Yes! But different from your thoughts." This also may seem like a "no," but it's really a disguised "yes." Watch carefully for God's answer.

"Yes! But more than you ever hoped or dreamed." What we ask for may be good and right, but God may choose to give us something even better. He sees the big picture and knows what is really good for us.

One more possible answer needs to be added: *"No! Not until you deal with that sin you are holding on to."* Even that is a gracious answer, for sin, remaining unconfessed and unforgiven, does great harm.

When God said "no" to Paul's request to remove his thorn in the flesh, it was with good reason. By allowing the thorn to remain, God taught Paul about his all-sufficient grace and about his "power made perfect in weakness." In the end Paul came to the point of delighting in weaknesses, insults, hardships, persecutions, and difficulties as he saw God's power doing more good through his weakness than Paul could ever do in his own strength (2 Corinthians 12:10).

Our confidence is not in prayer; it is in God. When prayer doesn't seem to work, it doesn't matter so much. God is still our Lord and Sustainer who graciously strengthens us.

Reflect

- Have you ever been disappointed in God for not answering your prayers? What are some reasons God may have had for not giving you what you asked for?
- Does it make sense to say, "Our confidence is not in prayer; it is in God"? Why?

Prayer-Starters for Praying 2 Corinthians 12:7-9

Praise God for his all-sufficient grace and power, which he uses on our behalf.

Confess any anger you may have toward God if you are disappointed in his way of answering or not answering your prayers.

Ask for wisdom to understand God's ways and grace to be able to "delight" in God's goodness, even if he says "no" to your requests.

Pray a blessing on your neighbors, using Ephesians 3:14-19:

Pray that they will be strengthened with power through the Spirit in their inner being.

Pray that Christ may dwell in their hearts through faith.

Pray that they may be rooted and established in God's love.

Pray that they will have power "to grasp how wide and long and high and deep is the love of Christ."

Pray that they "may be filled to the measure of all the fullness of God."

A SUGGESTION FOR MINISTRY ACTIVITY

Doorhangers

Now that you have prayed for *three weeks,* it's a good time to put out doorhangers. Doorhangers are a simple non-threatening way to let your neighbors know that you are praying for them. The doorhangers we use also invite your neighbors to call or stop by to give you specific prayer requests.

I suggest you use the simple *Announcement* doorhanger shown on the opposite page. You may have already received some with this book. If not, you can order them from HOPE Ministries.

You can place this doorhanger on your neighbor's door at any time. It's not necessary to meet them personally right away. Be sure to write your name, address, and phone number clearly on the doorhanger before putting it out. If you already know your neighbors well, and a doorhanger is too impersonal, just talk to them personally about your praying.

If you are praying for households that are at a distance, you may choose to send a prayer greeting card such as the one pictured on the opposite page.

If you're praying for work associates, an e-mail or a memo may be most appropriate. In a dormitory a simple hand-written note will do.

Four different doorhangers and six prayer greeting cards are available from HOPE Ministries. Call 800-217-5200 for more information or to order.

Announcement

A neighborhood *House of Prayer* is praying for you and your household—and this neighborhood. We are praying to God about things like health, employment, schooling, joy, peace, family harmony, good friendships, and spiritual blessings.

Is there some specific way we can pray for you or for someone you care about? Please call to let us know.

A praying friend: _____

Where I live: _____

To call me: _____

Greeting Cards

We've got you covered...

...with our prayers.

Praying for Others

DAY 1

What Is Intercession?

[Jesus] said to them, "Suppose one of you has a friend, and he goes to him at midnight and says, 'Friend, lend me three loaves of bread, because a friend of mine on a journey has come to me, and I have nothing to set before him.'

"Then the one inside answers, 'Don't bother me. The door is already locked, and my children are with me in bed. I can't get up and give you anything.' I tell you, though he will not get up and give him the bread because he is his friend, yet because of the man's boldness he will get up and give him as much as he needs."

Luke 11:5-8

When we move from petition (praying for ourselves) to intercession (praying for others), we are shifting the focus of prayer. We need to pray for ourselves so that we may receive all that God intends us to have. We also need to pray for others as an act of self-giving love.

The dictionary defines *intercession* as "acting between two parties; begging or pleading on behalf of another; mediating." An intercessor is a go-between, representing one party to another. In intercession, believers go before God and beseech him on behalf of others.

Jesus' story about the friend-in-the-middle portrays the role of the intercessor. This friend-in-the-middle has a friend-in-need who comes at midnight, and he has a friend-with-bread. Unable to meet the need of his midnight guest, this host goes to his other friend and pleads boldly and shamelessly till he receives what he needs. What he receives he carries back to his friend-in-need. He is a go-between.

The position of the friend-in-the-middle is the position of an intercessor, who pleads with one who has much on behalf of one who has nothing. In other words, intercessors labor before God—the Friend-with-Bread—and plead with him on behalf of those who need the Bread of heaven.

In the ongoing work of God, intercessory prayer is of prime importance. People desperately need our intercessory prayers. Many families are dysfunctional. Most churches are stagnated. Many neighborhoods are deteriorating. The majority of people do not have a saving knowledge of Jesus Christ. And they need far more than we are able to give them.

They need what only God can give. And God chooses to give his good gifts in response to the intercessory prayers of his people. That's where we come in. We can be friends-in-the-middle to God's lost and hurting world.

Reflect

- Who in your family, church, or neighborhood is like the friend who came at midnight? What kind of help do they need that is beyond your ability?
- What are you willing to do to see that they get what they need from God?

Prayer-Starters for Praying Luke 11:5-8

Praise God as the all-sufficient giver of every good gift.

Confess any failure on your part to intercede faithfully on behalf of needy persons around you.

Commit yourself to labor before God on behalf of your family, friends, neighbors, fellow workers, church members, and others.

Intercede right now on behalf of one or more needy persons whom God is bringing to mind.

Pray a BLESSing on those who live or work near you:

Body. Pray that God, who numbers the hairs of our head (Luke 12:7), will keep these persons from harm.

Labor. Since "all hard work brings a profit" (Proverbs 14:23), pray that they may be diligent in whatever work God has given them to do and that they are paid fairly.

Emotional. Pray that they may learn "to be content whatever the circumstances" of their lives are (Philippians 4:11).

Social. "As iron sharpens iron, so one man sharpens another" (Proverbs 27:17). Pray that they will have the kind of friends who will sharpen them.

Spiritual. Pray that they may "taste and see that the Lord is good" and be led to take refuge in him (Psalm 34:8).

DAY 2

God Seeks Intercessors

"I looked for a man among [Israel] who would build up the wall and stand before me in the gap on behalf of the land so I would not have to destroy it, but I found none. So I will pour out my wrath on them and consume them with my fiery anger, bringing down on their own heads all they have done, declares the Sovereign Lord."

Ezekiel 22:30-31 (also read vv. 23-30)

Several years ago I was making a determined effort to become a better intercessor. I tried to give it more time, cover more needs, and pray with greater intensity. For a while things went well. Soon, however, I found myself skipping these extended prayer times when it wasn't convenient. But it bothered me that I could skip prayer so easily.

When I asked the Lord for insight on this, he helped me see that my problem was that I didn't really believe intercession changed anything. It seemed that life went on normally around me whether I prayed or not.

Then God brought me to Ezekiel 22. He showed me that intercessors, who by means of their prayers "build up the wall and stand . . . in the gap," are absolutely crucial to his government of the world. When I asked the question of this passage, "Would the history of Israel have been different if God had found an intercessor?" I had to answer "yes." When I asked a further question, "Does the history of my family, church, or neighborhood depend on my intercession?" the answer again was "yes."

God seeks intercessors not because he lacks the wisdom or power to govern the world without them but because he, in his sovereign good pleasure, has chosen to govern the world through the prayers of his people. Intercession is not optional. It is a necessary and important part of God's way of working.

Things will happen when we pray that wouldn't have happened if we hadn't prayed. And things will not happen if we do not pray that would have happened if we had prayed.

In the New Testament era God the Father always finds an intercessor to "build up the wall and stand before [him] in the gap." The One he finds is Jesus Christ, who ever lives to make intercession. But Christ does not pray alone. Our intercessory prayers are coupled with his. And he, by means of his Spirit, prays through us.

No wonder the kingdom is advancing and the gospel is spreading to every nation in the world. It's because of prayer. Are your prayers contributing to this worldwide thrust?

Reflect

- Try to imagine God determining what will happen in your family, on your block, in your church, or in your nation on the basis of your prayers. How does that make you feel?
- What does that suggest about the importance of your role as an intercessor?

Prayer-Starters for Praying Ezekiel 22:30-31

Praise God for the greatness of his power and the wisdom of his choice to govern the world through the prayers of his people.

Confess any failure at intercession that you have now become aware of.

Thank God for the awesome privilege of ruling the world with him through your prayers of intercession.

Ask for grace to be a faithful intercessor.

Pray a BLESSing on those who live or work near you:

Body. Ask the heavenly Father, who feeds the birds of the air (Matthew 6:26), to supply the food needs of your neighbors.

Labor. Pray that employed neighbors will obey those who have authority over them with respect and sincerity of heart (Ephesians 6:5).

Emotional. Pray that they may keep their lives "free from the love of money and be content" with what they have (Hebrews 13:5).

Social. Pray for parents, asking that they will have the wisdom and ability to train up their children "in the way [they] should go" (Proverbs 22:6).

Spiritual. Pray that Satan will not be able to blind the minds of your neighbors and keep them from seeing "the light of the gospel of the glory of Christ" (2 Corinthians 4:4).

DAY 3

The Scope of Intercession

I urge, then, first of all, that requests, prayers, intercession and thanks-giving be made for everyone—for kings and all those in authority, that we may live peaceful and quiet lives in all godliness and holiness. This is good, and pleases God our Savior, who wants all men to be saved and to come to a knowledge of the truth.

1 Timothy 2:1-4

E. M. Bounds said, "Prayer can do anything God can do." That's true because the only power in prayer is the power of God. What's more, prayer can reach anywhere God can reach. And God is everywhere, so his power can reach to every corner of the earth through our prayers.

Two phrases in the above verses emphasize the broad scope of prayer: "for everyone" and "all men [persons]." Because God wants all persons "to be saved and to come to a knowledge of the truth," he urges us to pray for everyone.

Dr. O. Hallesby in his classic book *Prayer* grasps the heart of Paul's injunction: "It is our Lord's will that we who have received access to these powers through prayer should go through this world transmitting heavenly power to every corner of the world which needs it sorely. Our lives should be . . . quiet but steadily flowing streams of blessing, which through our prayers and intercessions should reach our whole environment" (p. 64).

When I sit in my favorite chair for my morning devotions, I imagine my prayers ascending to the throne room of heaven, and I imagine God, in response, moving his hands in the places where my prayers direct. I imagine his power being released on the west coast as I pray for family members, in our nation's capitol as I pray for government officials, in foreign lands as I pray for mission enterprises, and in the homes and hearts of my neighbors as I pray for them. My prayers can release a blessing or bring change anywhere in the world without my moving from that chair. What an awesome power God has given us!

Though God would have us pray broad intercessory prayers, our prayer responsibilities start close to home. Our first responsibility is for immediate family members, then relatives and friends, then the spiritual family in which God has placed us, and then beyond that to our neighbors, community, nation, and world.

If our prayers focus only on those who are nearby, we have not caught the scope of what God intends through prayer. If they focus mainly on those far away, we may be guilty of failing to provide for our immediate families and of denying the faith (1 Timothy 5:4, 8).

Reflect

- Imagine your prayers transmitting heavenly power to every corner of the world. Think of some of those people and places.
- Imagine persons experiencing the joy of being saved and coming to a knowledge of the truth as a result of your prayers.

Prayer-Starters for Praying 1 Timothy 2:1-4

Praise God, who is everywhere present in the universe.

If your prayers have been narrow and limited, *confess* that failure to God.

Thank God for the breadth and depth of his concern for this world.

Commit yourself to make "requests, prayers, intercession and thanksgiving . . . for everyone," including "kings and all those in authority."

Pray some broad prayers, using the following Bible verses. Remember, though, that the nations begin at your doorstep:

Pray that through Jesus Christ "all nations on earth will be blessed," as God promised Abraham in Genesis 22:18.

Pray that "all the ends of the earth will remember and turn to the Lord, and all the families of the nations will bow down before him" (Psalm 22:27).

Pray that Isaiah 9:2—"The people walking in darkness have seen a great light; on those living in the land of the shadow of death a light has dawned"— will become a reality in lands that are still in the darkness of false religions.

Pray that "every tongue [will] confess that Jesus Christ is Lord, to the glory of God the Father" (Philippians 2:11).

DAY 4

Interceding for Those Who Can't Pray for Themselves

The LORD . . . said to Eliphaz the Temanite, "I am angry with you and your two friends . . . . Go to my servant Job and sacrifice a burnt offering for yourselves. My servant Job will pray for you, and I will accept his prayer and not deal with you according to your folly. . . . And the LORD accepted Job's prayer."

Job 42:7-9

Several recent polls in North America show that about 80 percent of the population do not have a saving relationship with Jesus Christ. That means they do not regularly have access to God's throne of grace. They may try to pray, but they cannot get through to God, since access to the throne is only through Jesus Christ.

That is a horrible, hopeless state to be in—cut off from the One who is the source of all grace and blessing. That was the state in which Eliphaz and his friends found themselves, at least temporarily, when God came to them and said, "My servant Job will pray for you, and I will accept his prayer." This was God's way of saying, "I won't listen to your prayers. You don't have access. You'd better get Job to pray for you."

The word in the Greek language that our Bibles translate as *intercession* means "having freedom of access." It was originally a technical term that meant meeting with a king in order to make a request. In the Bible *intercession* means seeking the presence and attention of God on behalf of others.

The privilege of access is given to believers not simply so that we may ask for ourselves but also so that we may ask for others, especially those who have no access. God has so much to give them but, having determined long ago to give in response to asking, he withholds his gracious giving until we intercede.

When believers begin to pray seriously for their neighbors, things begin to happen. When members of a church planted a *House of Prayer* in an apartment complex to pray for those who lived there, the manager became a Christian, drug dealers moved out, crime rates went down, many tenants started going to church, several Bible studies started, and ten people made commitments to Christ. The difference was so evident that the police, discovering the reason for the changes, asked the church to consider planting similar *Houses of Prayer* in other complexes.

What do you think God wants to see happen in the lives of the people around you? Are you willing to be the one to intercede so that God may accomplish his will in your neighborhood through your prayers?

Reflect

- What would it be like to be a non-Christian who had no one to pray for you?
- Consider what it would mean to you to live in a neighborhood in which believers in *Light-Houses of Prayer* prayed regularly for you.

Prayer-Starters for Praying Job 42:7-9

Thank God for the privilege of access to his throne, opened up for you through Jesus Christ.

If you have failed to use your privilege of access to the throne on behalf of unsaved persons, *confess* this sin to God and claim his forgiving grace.

Tell God of your readiness to be a faithful intercessor, and *ask* his help in doing so.

Seek God's guidance in praying for some persons or families who cannot or do not pray for themselves:

Envision each person or family for whom you are interceding. Ask God to reveal to you, as you hold them in your mind's eye, what he wants to accomplish in their lives. Be still before God and wait patiently before him. Pray for the things he brings to mind.

DAY 5

Interceding for the Unsaved

Brothers, my heart's desire and prayer to God for the Israelites is that they may be saved.

Romans 10:1

The Bible clearly requires us to pray for persons who are not saved. In 1 Timothy 2 we are reminded that God wants all persons to be saved, and we are urged "therefore" to pray for everyone. Jesus modeled prayer for the unsaved when he prayed, "My prayer is not for [my disciples] alone. I pray also for those who will believe in me through their message" (John 17:20). And the apostle Paul was praying for the unsaved when he prayed his heart's desire for the Israelites (Romans 10:1).

How should we pray for those who are not saved?

First, we should pray that *the unsaved will be drawn by the Father.* Jesus said, "No one can come to me unless the Father who sent me draws him" (John 6:44).

Second, we should pray that *those who hear the gospel will understand it.* Jesus warns that the evil one will come and snatch away the gospel seed sown in a person's heart if it is not understood (Matthew 13:19). The spiritual understanding and enlightenment required must come from God, who is moved to respond to the prayers of his people.

Third, we should pray that *unbelievers' eyes will be opened so that they can see the light.* As we pray this prayer, we will once again be contending with the adversary, "the god of this age [who] has blinded the minds of unbelievers, so that they cannot see the light of the gospel of the glory of Christ" (2 Corinthians 4:4). Opening spiritual eyes is, of course, God's business. But releasing God's power to open blinded eyes is prayer business, to which God calls us.

God honors prayer for the unsaved. A *House of Prayer* prayed for a young man who had run away from home and joined a gang. The young man returned home and made a commitment to Christ. Later his grandfather gave his life to Christ, also in response to prayer.

Another *House of Prayer* saw four families come to the Lord after eight months of weekly meetings to pray for their neighbors.

This is prayer-evangelism; evangelism in which God moves in the hearts and lives of people in response to the earnest prayers of believers. Who among those who will believe in Christ are you praying for?

Reflect

- Do you care enough about the unsaved to pray earnestly for their salvation?
- Would you care more if it were your own children or family members who were unsaved? Remember that all unsaved persons are wayward sons and daughters of God's family. God does not want "anyone to perish, but everyone to come to repentance" (2 Peter 3:9).

Prayer-Starters for Praying Romans 10:1

Praise God, who "so loved the world that he gave his one and only Son, that whoever believes in him shall . . . have eternal life" (John 3:16).

Thank God for those who prayed for you and helped to open the door of salvation for you.

If you do not have a burden for the unsaved, *ask* God to put such a burden on your heart.

Commit yourself to partner with Jesus Christ in praying for those yet to be saved.

Pray for unsaved persons, using the following Bible verses:

Ask the Father to draw these persons to himself (John 6:44).

Ask God to give them an understanding of the gospel and to forbid the devil from snatching away what is sown in their hearts (Matthew 13:19).

Ask God to open their spiritual eyes, since "the god of this age has blinded the minds of unbelievers" (2 Corinthians 4:4).

Pray for opportunities to relate to your neighbors in which you are able to "be wise in the way you act toward outsiders" and to "make the most of every opportunity," with "your conversation . . . always full of grace, seasoned with salt, so that you may know how to answer everyone" (Colossians 4:5-6).

A SUGGESTION FOR MINISTRY ACTIVITY

Personal Contact

By now you have prayed for your neighbors for *four weeks*. You've laid a foundation of prayer and prepared the way for a personal contact.

Make a personal contact, if you don't have a relationship already, by knocking on your neighbors' doors, introducing yourself, mentioning your *Light-House of Prayer*, and asking for prayer suggestions. Move from impersonal questions to personal questions as in the following sequence:

"Are you aware of needs in this neighborhood that we should pray about?"
"Are there concerns among your family or friends that we can pray about?"
"Is there some way we can pray for you?"

Make a note of your neighbors' suggestions as they give them, and ask your neighbors to let you know when there is change for the better. This will help convince them that you are serious about praying for them.

Before you leave, ask if it's okay for you to contact them again to get new prayer requests or learn about answers to prayer. Leave a calling card with them that gives them your name, address, and phone number and spells out why and how you pray.

See the following two pages for samples of our *Contact Card* and *Calling Card*.

Contact Card

CONTACT CARD

_____

Person Contacted

_____

Date Contacted

"I'm part of a group that is praying regularly for this (neighborhood, office, workplace, dormitory, etc.). It's called a (House of Prayer). Would you be willing to give us your input so that we can pray more specifically?"

1. "Are you aware of needs or concerns in this (neighborhood, office, workplace, dormitory, etc.) that you think we should pray about?"

2. "Are there needs or concerns among your family or friends that we can pray about?"

3. "Is there some way we can pray for you?"

HOPE MINISTRIES • P.O. BOX 141312 • GRAND RAPIDS, MI • 49514 • 800-217-5200

Calling Card

_____

Name

_____

Address

_____

Telephone

A *House of Prayer* is a place where believers pray for their neighbors.

We pray because . . .
- prayer is the shortest way to God.
- prayer honors God, who is eager to have us ask.
- prayer is the means by which heaven's blessings are brought down to earth.
- prayer changes things which need to be changed.
- prayer is powerful and effective (James 5:16).

We pray for . . .
- physical blessings like health, jobs, and income.
- inner-world blessings like joy and peace.
- relational blessings like love, family harmony, and good friends.
- spiritual blessings like faith, hope, and peace with God.
- solutions to life's problems.

HOPE MINISTRIES • P.O. BOX 141312 • GRAND RAPIDS, MI • 49514 • (800) 217-5200

The Difference Prayer Makes

Prayer Releases God's Power

The prayer of a righteous man is powerful and effective.
Elijah was a man just like us. He prayed earnestly that it would not
rain, and it did not rain on the land for three and a half years. Again he
prayed, and the heavens gave rain, and the earth produced its crops.

James 5:16-18

"Prayer," said C. Samuel Storms, "in and of itself possesses no power." I was astounded by that, and I didn't understand it until I read what Storms said next: "Prayer is powerful because God is powerful, and prayer is the means through which that divine power is released and channeled into our lives" (*Reaching God's Ear,* p. 223). In other words, all the power in prayer is really God's power activated by prayer.

When you pray for another person, there is nothing that flows from you to them—no vibes, no force, no energy. Instead, your prayers go heavenward, and the power of God moves from him to the ones you pray for.

When the Bible says "prayer is powerful and effective," it means God acts powerfully and effectively through the prayers of his people. Prayer is the instrument by which God has chosen to have his power directed in the universe. O. Hallesby provides something of a mental picture of how this works: "This power is so rich and so mobile that all we have to do when we pray is to point to the persons or things to which we desire to have this power applied, and He, the Lord of this power, will direct the necessary power to the desired place" (*Prayer,* p. 63). What a surprising arrangement—God partnering with human beings to accomplish his purposes!

R. A. Torrey, enthralled by the enormity of this power, states, "Prayer is the key that unlocks all the storehouses of God's infinite grace and power. All that God is, and . . . has, is at the disposal of prayer. Prayer can do anything that God can do, and as God can do any thing, prayer is omnipotent" (*The Power of Prayer,* p. 17).

Prayer can do what political action cannot, what education cannot, what military might cannot, and what planning committees cannot. All these are impotent by comparison.

Prayer can move mountains. It can change human hearts, families, neighborhoods, cities, and nations. It's the ultimate source of power, because it is the power of Almighty God.

This power is available to the humblest Christian. It was "a man just like us" who prayed "that it would not rain," and God stopped the rain in Israel for three and a half years. Where will the power of your prayers be felt today?

Reflect
- Where do you think God would like some of that power directed through your prayers today?
- What do you think he would like to do in your neighborhood in response to prayer?

Prayer-Starters for Praying James 5:16-18
Praise God for the great power by which he moves in this world and governs the affairs of all people.

Thank God for his willingness to have us direct his power to places and persons through prayer.

Confess if you have failed to make use of the great privilege to advance God's cause in this world.

Ask God to help you become a powerful and effective "pray-er" in the future.

Pray a BLESSing on those who live or work near you:
Body. Thank God for his generous provision. "Give thanks to the Lord, for he . . . . gives food to every creature. His love endures forever" (Psalm 136:1, 25).

Labor. Pray that your neighbors may learn to work, doing something useful with their hands so that they "may have something to share with those in need" (Ephesians 4:28).

Emotional. Pray that God will give them the "perfect peace" that comes from a steadfast mind and a trusting heart (Isaiah 26:3).

Social. Pray that they may be sensitive to the needs of others around them and will have a desire to help and care for them.

Spiritual. Pray that the Holy Spirit, who is sent to convict the world of sin, righteousness, and judgment (John 16:8), will work powerfully and effectively in the hearts and lives of unsaved people you pray for.

DAY 2

The Key to Great Works

"I tell you the truth, anyone who has faith in me will do what I have been doing. He will do even greater things than these, because I am going to the Father. And I will do whatever you ask in my name, so that the Son may bring glory to the Father."

John 14:12-14

Jesus spoke these words shortly before he was arrested and crucified. He had just told his disciples he would be leaving them. This news left them confused and fearful—confused about the future of the work and fearful that they would not be able to do it.

Jesus' words were intended to allay the disciples' fears. He assured them that they *would be able* to do the work. In fact, they would do what he had been doing—and even greater things.

On the face of it this seems a preposterous thing for Jesus to say. After all, he had preached great sermons, attracted huge crowds, spoken wonderful words of wisdom, walked on water, stilled a storm, healed the sick, and raised the dead. How could the disciples possibly do such things?

Jesus explains that it would be possible because he was going to the Father and they would be able to ask in his name for what they needed in order to do the work of God's kingdom.

His *going* to the Father meant that he would be given all power in heaven and on earth. Thus empowered, he would continue his work on earth in a different way—through them.

Their *asking* in his name would link him to them. By means of prayer his power would be at their disposal as they carried on his ministry "to the ends of the earth" (Acts 1:8). Prayer would be "the talking part" of this ministry partnership in which he would supply the power and they would do the work.

These words of Jesus, though meant to comfort and encourage his first disciples, were also meant for us. Jesus, you will notice, addressed these surprising words to "anyone who has faith in me." That includes you, if you are a Christian, and me.

What a powerful combination: Christ on the throne of the universe, empowering us, his disciples, here on earth to build his kingdom. We ask, and he acts, and the work gets done—great works to the glory of God the Father.

What's Jesus doing through you today?

Reflect

- Have most of your prayers been for things that build the kingdom of God, or have they been somewhat more selfish?
- What things might the ascended Christ want to accomplish through you?
- Is there some place where you see great things happening in the body of Christ today?

Prayer-Starters for Praying John 14:12-14

Praise Christ for the mighty works he did while he was personally on earth and for the mighty works he has accomplished through his disciples since that day.

Confess if you find that your prayers have been selfishly motivated and not ministry oriented.

Thank Christ that he is available to hear and answer your prayers brought in his name.

Identify some "great things" Christ might want to do for the glory of the Father, and begin to *ask* him to do them.

Pray for your neighbors and co-workers using the pattern of the Lord's Prayer:

Pray that God's name will be hallowed in and through their lives.

Pray that God's kingdom will be established in their surroundings and Satan's works destroyed.

Pray that they will be led to know and do God's will as do the angels in heaven.

Pray that God will supply their daily needs.

Pray that God will forgive their sins.

Pray that God will keep them from temptation and protect them from the evil one.

DAY 3

The Strength to Stand

Pray in the Spirit on all occasions with all kinds of prayers and requests. With this in mind, be alert and always keep on praying for all the saints.

Ephesians 6:18

God has given us prayer so that we may help each other stand. The devil is always scheming to cause us to fall. But God provides ways to help us stand victorious over the powers of evil.

Paul warns us in Ephesians 6 against the devil's schemes and the "powers of this dark world" that are constantly opposing us. Four times he uses the word "stand" to encourage us to hold out against the onslaughts of the "spiritual forces of evil" (Ephesians 6:11-14).

Standing our ground requires that we first "put on the full armor of God." We are protected against the devil by knowing the truth, being righteous, having the gospel of peace, trusting God, possessing salvation, and using the word of God in the right way. But Paul's order to "put on the full armor" does not end with "take . . . the sword of the Spirit, which is the word of God." It goes on without a break to say, "Pray in the Spirit on all occasions." In other words, the prayer support we give each other is an important part of our defense against the devil.

The prayer support required is all-embracing. It's "on *all* occasions," of "*all* kinds," "*always*," and "for *all* the saints." Imagine being in the midst of a fellowship of Christians who prayed for each other this way. The possibility of falling would surely be minimized.

Paul, practicing what he preached, often prayed that way for his friends in Christ. For example, to the Colossians he wrote, "We have not stopped . . . asking God to fill you with the knowledge of his will through all spiritual wisdom and understanding. And we pray this in order that you may live a life worthy of the Lord and may please him in every way: bearing fruit in every good work, growing in the knowledge of God, being strengthened with all power according to his glorious might so that you may have great endurance and patience" (Colossians 1:9-11). Wouldn't you like to have Paul as your prayer partner? It's not hard to imagine that kind of prayer support making a difference.

God's intent is that *all* believers be strengthened to stand, as *all* take seriously the responsibility to *always* keep on praying, on *all* occasions, with *all* kinds of prayer, for *all* the saints.

That's a tall order. It goes far beyond the kind of casual praying that most Christians are accustomed to. It calls for commitment.

Reflect

- Do you sense that you are getting the kind of prayer support you need in order to stand?
- Are you giving those around you the kind of prayer support they need in order to stand?
- Is there anything more you should be doing to support those around you in prayer? Be as specific as possible.

Prayer-Starters for Praying Ephesians 6:18

Thank God for his wise plan to supply spiritual prayer support for you. Thank him for those who have given you prayer support.

Confess any failure you are aware of as you reflect on this passage.

Ask God to help the community of believers of which you are a part to live up to the standard of Ephesians 6:18.

Commit yourself to serious prayer support for those around you.

Pray a BLESSing on those who live or work near you:

Body. Pray that God will provide for your neighbors, just as he "makes grass grow for the cattle, and plants . . . to cultivate—bringing forth food from the earth" (Psalm 104:14).

Labor. Pray that their work may give them a sense of satisfaction. "The sleep of a laborer is sweet, whether he eats little or much" (Ecclesiastes 5:12).

Emotional. Pray that they may be content because they have "learned the secret of being content in any and every situation, whether well fed or hungry, whether living in plenty or in want" (Philippians 4:12).

Social. Pray that they may "be kind and compassionate to one another, forgiving each other" (Ephesians 4:32).

Spiritual. Pray that they will "put aside the deeds of darkness and put on the armor of light" (Romans 13:12).

DAY 4

Prayer Defeats Satan

"Simon, Simon, Satan has asked to sift you as wheat. But I have prayed for you, Simon, that your faith may not fail. And when you have turned back, strengthen your brothers."

Luke 22:31-32

There are two powerful forces at work in the world today—the power of God and the power of Satan. The power of God is infinitely greater, but we are affected by both.

Satan, bent on our destruction, goes about "like a roaring lion looking for someone to devour" (1 Peter 5:8). God, bent on our salvation, supplies "everything we need for life and godliness" (2 Peter 1:3).

Since Satan's power is greater than ours, we are constantly at risk. Paul reminds us that we struggle "against the rulers, against the authorities, against the powers of this dark world and against the spiritual forces of evil" (Ephesians 6:12). But since God's power is greater than Satan's, we are safe. He is our constant source of protection.

Prayer is the God-given means by which God's power is brought to our defense so that we are able to stand up against the devil's schemes. When Peter was being severely tested by Satan, Jesus came to his defense with prayer. He said, "I have prayed for you, Simon, that your faith may not fail."

We are engaged in a war that we must fight on our knees. Prayer is the power by which we are equipped to overcome the devil. To face him in our own strength is folly and a sure pathway to defeat.

The devil dreads our prayers more than anything else. A mighty prayer warrior once said, "Do you realize that there is nothing the devil dreads so much as prayer? His great concern is to keep us from praying. He loves to see us 'up to our eyes' in work—provided we do not pray. He does not fear if we are eager Bible students—provided we are little in prayer. Someone has wisely said, 'Satan laughs at our toiling, mocks at our wisdom, but trembles when we pray'" (*The Kneeling Christian, p. 17*).

It's no wonder that Satan trembles. By means of prayer the power of the omnipotent God of heaven and earth is brought against him. He doesn't stand a chance.

By prayer the kingdom of God is built, and by prayer the kingdom of Satan is destroyed. Where there is no prayer, there are no great works and there is no building of the kingdom. Let there be prayer so that God may be glorified and his kingdom may come in all its fullness.

Reflect
- To what extent are you conscious that your prayers bring defeat to Satan's efforts?
- Who among your acquaintances is now being tested by Satan and in need of your prayers?

Prayer-Starters for Praying Luke 22:31-32

Praise the omnipotent God, who is able to destroy the works of the devil and protect his children.

Ask Christ to teach you how to make use of prayer as a weapon to defeat Satan and help to advance God's kingdom.

Commit yourself to prayerfully support those around you, especially those whom you sense are under attack.

Pray for those who live or work near you, asking that God will set them free from the powers of evil:

Ask God to set them free from bondage so that "they will come to their senses and escape from the trap of the devil, who has taken them captive to do his will" (2 Timothy 2:26).

Pray that God will "open their eyes and turn them from darkness to light, and from the power of Satan to God, so that they may receive forgiveness of sins and a place among those who are sanctified by faith in [Jesus]" (Acts 26:18).

Pray that the Son of God, who came "to destroy the devil's work" (1 John 3:8), may do so among your neighbors or fellow workers.

DAY 5

Prayer Shapes History

Another angel, who had a golden censer, came and stood at the altar.
He was given much incense to offer, with the prayers of all the saints,
on the golden altar before the throne. The smoke of the incense, togeth-
er with the prayers of the saints, went up before God from the angel's
hand. Then the angel took the censer, filled it with fire from the altar,
and hurled it on the earth; and there came peals of thunder, rumblings,
flashes of lightning and an earthquake.

Revelation 8:3-5

Do you get the picture here? The prayers of saints, accumulated throughout the ages on the altar of prayer, await the day when God acts on them. The day finally comes when those prayers are brought out and answered. Hurled upon the earth, they bring about cataclysmic changes that mark the beginnings of the end of history.

Can you find yourself in the picture? You can if you have ever prayed for the coming of Christ, or if you have ever prayed that wrongs will someday be made right. Your prayers, with those of billions of other believers, will one day be answered when God brings an end to the world and establishes his glorious kingdom.

God's memory is perfect. He never forgets a prayer. Have you ever noticed that God sometimes answers prayers long after you have stopped praying them? He takes every prayer, prayed in the name of his Son, seriously—even those that were prayed centuries ago.

Today, according to statistician David Barret, there are approximately 170 million believers praying for the revival of the church and world evangelization. There are 10 million small groups praying weekly for spiritual awakening and for the completion of the Great Commission. God has heard every one of these prayers and will answer them all according to his promise and his purpose. What a day that will be!

The prayers of the saints shape history. History was shaped when Moses, from a hillside, lifted up his hands in intercession over a battlefield (Exodus 17:8-13). History was shaped when Elijah prayed "that it would not rain"; there was famine for three and a half years in Israel (James 5:16). History was shaped when early Christians prayed until the wee hours of the morning and Peter miraculously escaped from prison (Acts 12:1-17).

In a sense "the future of the world is in the hands of praying Christians." So is the future of your neighborhood and the future of your church, if you are a praying Christian. I hope and pray that your prayers will contribute to a glorious future for the kingdom of God right where you live—and to a still more glorious future in days to come.

Reflect

- Do you dare to believe that the lives of loved ones you pray for are being shaped through your prayers?
- How about the history of your church? Your neighborhood? Your nation? How much are your prayers contributing to the work of God in them?

Prayer-Starters for Praying Revelation 8:3-5

Praise God as the Ruler of the nations, the One ultimately in charge of history.

Thank God for hearing your prayers and answering them when the time is right.

Ask God's forgiveness if your prayers have been so weak as to contribute almost nothing to the shaping of history.

Commit yourself to faithful, fervent prayer.

Pray for those who live or work near you, asking that they will . . .

"Seek the Lord while he may be found" and "call on him while he is near," forsaking wicked ways and evil thoughts and turning to the Lord, coming to know him personally, that "he will freely pardon" (Isaiah 55:6-7).

Pray that, in bringing history to an end . . .

"The Sovereign Lord will wipe away the tears from all faces; he will remove the disgrace of his people from all the earth" (Isaiah 25:8).

How Do I Care for My Neighbors?

by

Edith Bajema

John F. DeVries

Alvin J. Vander Griend

Contents

Love Is the Foundation

DAY 1

Loving God First

*"'Love the Lord your God with all your heart and with all your soul
and with all your mind.' This is the first and greatest commandment.
And the second is like it: 'Love your neighbor as yourself.'"*

Matthew 22:37-39

Have you ever wondered why you are on this planet? What plan does God have for you? Is there some larger purpose than making as good a living as possible, raising a family, making ends meet?

You bet there is! And Jesus summarizes that whole plan in one statement: *Love God and love your neighbor.* These are the two callings in your life. They are meant to be the foundation of all you do.

In the next five weeks of devotional readings this book will help you focus on the second great commandment: loving your neighbor as yourself. But notice that this commandment flows from and is secondary to the first: loving God with all your heart.

Why is it important to love God with all your heart? Because if you are not close to the heart of God, you will not feel the strength and passion of God's love for your neighbors.

Let me illustrate with a story. Several years ago my son and I saw a small kitten on a farm, a "barn cat." It was bone-thin, with a swollen belly and infected eyes. Filled with pity for the little creature, and knowing it would not get medical treatment on the farm, we asked the farmer's permission to take it home.

The kitten was terrified. When we got home that evening, we made a large, secure box for it, filled with soft rags. We left it outside, covered, planning to take it to the vet in the morning.

That night I woke to the sound of thunder and pouring rain. I ran outside to bring the box under shelter—only to find the cover open and the box empty! I searched everywhere, not caring about the rain. All I could think of was a small, terrified kitten.

An hour later, I crawled back into bed, defeated. "Lord," I prayed over and over, "please help the kitten to be safe. Please don't let it wander away and starve. Save its life and help me to find it."

Then God spoke to my heart. "This is how I feel about your neighbors," he said. "I have the same passionate concern to save them from death. Do you have the same love for your neighbors as you do for that lost kitten?"

80

God taught me a powerful lesson that night. I could pray fervently for a lost kitten—but could I love my lost neighbors and pray fervently for them? I knew that if I were to love my neighbor, it would come through my drawing close enough to God's heart to feel his passion for them.

How close are you to God's heart? Do you love God enough to allow him to put his heart into yours? Are you willing to open yourself in prayer to receive God's heart for your neighbors? These next few weeks of devotions will challenge to you do that. But it will mean opening your heart to God first.

—EB

Reflect/Act

- How often do you think about the two great commandments during your day? What can you do to think about them more?
- How can you grow in loving God "with all your heart and with all your soul and with all your mind"?
- How can you grow in loving your neighbor as yourself?

Prayer-Starters for Praying Matthew 22:37-39

Praise God for his desire to have a love relationship with you.

Confess any failure on your part to love God with all your heart and soul and mind, and ask him to remove things that get in the way of your loving him fully.

Thank God for the compassionate love in his heart for you and for each person in your home and on your street.

Ask God to draw you close enough to his heart to feel his passionate concern and overwhelming desire to save your neighbors from spiritual separation from him. Ask God to teach you how to love your neighbors as you love yourself and your family.

Pray a BLESSing on those who live or work near you:

Body. Pray that God will make you aware of any physical limitations or illnesses your neighbors may have. Then ask God to use you to show his love in that circumstance or need.

Labor. Pray that neighbors who work outside the home will meet Christians who show them the deep and passionate love of God.

Emotional. Ask God to fill the empty spaces in unsaved neighbors' hearts with the knowledge that there is a God who loves them and wants them to love him in return.

Social. Ask the Holy Spirit to make you sensitive to neighbors who may be looking for someone to talk to. Then ask the Spirit to teach you how to reach out in love to them.

Spiritual. Pray that those who live on your street will be "rooted and established" in God's love and "have power . . . to grasp how wide and long and high and deep is the love of Christ" (Ephesians 3:17-18).

DAY 2

The Greatest Thing

If I have the gift of prophecy and can fathom all mysteries and all knowledge, and if I have a faith that can move mountains, but have not love, I am nothing. If I give all I possess to the poor and surrender my body to the flames, but have not love, I gain nothing.

1 Corinthians 13:2-3

Today we might say these verses in a different way: "If I am successful at my job and have a great bank account and lots of material possessions, but have not love, I am worth nothing. If I work in many community organizations and donate time and money to worthy causes, but have not love, it gains me nothing."

What is the greatest thing in your life? It's your capacity to love.

Sometimes Christians today think the greatest thing is their ability to do good things or to give sums of money to worthy causes. But that's not the case. Greater than any of these things is to give and show love.

What is love? The apostle Paul gives us some ideas: "Love is patient, love is kind. It does not envy, it does not boast, it is not proud. It is not rude, it is not self-seeking, it is not easily angered, it keeps no record of wrongs. . . . It always protects, always trusts, always hopes, always perseveres" (1 Corinthians 13:4-7).

This generous spirit of love is the greatest thing in your life as a Christian. Without it, your faith is meaningless. Without it, your deeds are meaningless.

In this five-week set of devotions you will be encouraged to reach out to your neighbors with good and caring deeds. You will be challenged to find ways to share your faith with them. But without the kind, patient, protective, trusting, hopeful, persevering spirit of love in your heart toward them, your actions and words will be "only a resounding gong or a clanging cymbal" (1 Corinthians 13:1).

So before you reach out to the people who live on your street, do an attitude check. What is your motive for reaching out? Do you see your offer simply as an act of duty, or is there true affection and concern for the person you are reaching?

God knows, of course, how human and frail we are. Our love for another person will never be perfect on this earth. God is not asking us to produce and manufacture a perfect love for others in our hearts. He is asking us to join our hearts to his love, to receive his love and let it flow through us. "We love because he first loved us" (1 John 4:19).

This series of devotions asks, "How do I care for my neighbors?" The answer is, first of all, to love them from the heart, as God does. And when you do that, you are giving them the greatest thing on earth.

—EB

Reflect/Act

- Has anyone ever done you a favor—but with an uncaring attitude toward you? How did that feel?
- Make yourself available in this coming week for God's love to flow through you to another person.

Prayer-Starters for Praying 1 Corinthians 13:2-3

Praise God for showing you what love is: "This is how we know what love is: Jesus Christ laid down his life for us" (1 John 3:16).

Confess any failings in which you may have shown that giving and receiving God's love were not the "main thing" in your life.

Ask God to change your perspective in life—your aims, goals, and desires—to be more like his, so that you value love as highly as God does.

Thank God for giving you neighbors with whom you can share his love.

Pray a BLESSing on those who live or work near you:

Body. Ask God to take care of your neighbors' physical needs this week, particularly any needs aggravated by loneliness, depression, or despair.

Labor. Ask God to help your neighbors see that there are things more important than money, possessions, or career, and to help them make God's love the "main thing" in their lives—even in the workplace.

Emotional. Pray for neighbors who may suffer from loneliness because they have made other things more important in their lives.

Social. Pray that the Holy Spirit will help your neighbors to find time for the relationships that are important to them, especially between parents and children.

Spiritual. Ask God to draw your neighbors into his love so that they may find the greatest treasure in life—love.

DAY 3

The Love That Never Fails

Love never fails. But where there are prophecies, they will cease; where there are tongues, they will be stilled; where there is knowledge, it will pass away. For we know in part and we prophesy in part, but when perfection comes, the imperfect disappears.

1 Corinthians 13:8-10

There aren't many things in life about which you can say, "It never fails." A battery company claims to have a battery that never fails. Their untiring little bunny—the Energizer Bunny—goes on, and on, and on. But making a claim about something doesn't make it so. Media commercials and reality are two different things.

The apostle Paul's claim about love, though, is firmly rooted in reality. Love—the Bible's kind of love—doesn't fail. It doesn't fail because it is of God, whose nature is to love. God's love is different than human kinds of love. God's love flows to people who don't deserve it—unworthy people. It makes the ultimate sacrifice for them. "While we were still sinners, Christ died for us," says Paul in Romans 5:8.

When the apostle says, "Love never fails," he's not talking only about God's love; he's also talking about God's love *in us* and *through us.* Paul is reminding us that it's possible for us, with the love of God in our hearts, to love as God loves. Lewis Smedes defines this love as "the power that moves you to give to another person with no expectation of reward." Such love doesn't fail because it is not based on another person's behavior. Human love says, "I will keep loving you as long as you meet my needs, as long as you are well-behaved, as long as you live up to my expectations." "Love that never fails" does not allow the behavior of another human being to interrupt its commitment to a life of love.

This is the way God expects us to relate to our neighbors, with never-failing love—a love that blesses, lifts, cares, and serves. There's power in that kind of love, a power that touches people's hearts and lives. It's power that flows from God to us and through us to those whom we love. It's energized love. It cannot be stopped. It goes on, and on, and on.

A life of love is the only life truly worth living. A life without love amounts to nothing—"nothing but the creaking of a rusty gate" (*The Message,* 1 Corinthians 13:1).

You and I must first receive this kind of love from God. Then we are in a position to devote the rest of our lives to cultivating and freely giving this "love that never fails" to those around us.

—AVG

Reflect/Act

• Take time today to read 1 Corinthians 13 and consider what never-failing love means in your relations to neighbors, work associates, and fellow students.

• Think of one thing you can do to bless, lift, or serve a friend or neighbor.

Prayer-Starters for Praying 1 Corinthians 13:8-10

Praise God for his never-failing love to us.

Confess the inadequacy of the conditional types of love we often show to the people around us.

Thank God for people who, with never-failing love, have not given up on you.

Commit yourself to living a life of never-failing love.

Pray a BLESSing on those who live or work near you:

Body. Pray for neighbors who may be slaves to an addiction. Ask that God will restore them to freedom from whatever holds them in bondage and cripples their lives.

Labor. Pray for neighbors who may feel useless because they are unable to work. Ask God to help them focus on what they still can do, and to show them that our worth is not found in what we do but in who we are.

Emotional. Pray for lonely people whose life situations make them feel isolated. Ask God to help you draw them into vibrant friendship with Jesus Christ.

Social. Pray for parents whose responsibilities sometimes seem overwhelming, that they may receive the help they need to be good parents.

Spiritual. Pray that neighbors may, by the grace of God, come to treasure the Lord and love him with all their heart, soul, and mind.

DAY 4

Loving with Actions

Let us not love with words or tongue but with actions and in truth.
1 John 3:18

I saw a newly widowed man in our church standing in the fellowship hall after worship. Though he was surrounded by people, I could sense a feeling of loneliness and pain in his bearing. He looked thinner than he was six months ago, when his wife was still alive.

My heart was moved with compassion and respect for this retired pastor, whose wife had been a true example of grace and godliness. How he must be missing her, I thought. Is there something I can do? I went over to him.

We exchanged greetings and talked about the weather. Then I said, "Rev. Jones, I know it must be a hard time for you, and you must miss Jane very much. I know that others here have said they miss her too; she was a very loving and godly person."

He acknowledged that he was having a difficult time, and I wanted to offer something to let him know that others cared about him. "I'll be praying for you," I said. "Every day." He shook my hand, truly grateful.

"Thank you," he said. "You don't know how much it means to have people praying—even just a few words a day. It makes such a difference."

Two weeks later I saw him at church again and remembered our conversation. I also remembered, to my embarrassment and guilt, that I had not kept my promise to pray for him every day. Perhaps once or twice I had done so, but then I had let it slip. I had found it much easier to make the offer than to put it into action.

Have you ever found yourself in the same situation—promising to do something good for a friend or neighbor and then not carrying through? The words are easy. The actions are hard.

It's easy to say to a bereaved neighbor, "We should get together sometime." Or to a new neighbor, "We'd like to have you over for dinner (or coffee or dessert) soon." Or to a neighbor sick with cancer, "I'd love to bring a pot of soup over sometime." Or to a neighbor working on a difficult project, "I'll stop by sometime and give you a hand."

Saying words that sound good is easy—so easy, in fact, that they are quickly forgotten by the person who speaks them. Of course, the words are spoken with good intentions; good intentions feel good in our hearts. But they don't do the other person any good unless they're accompanied by action. That's John's point in his letter. "Put feet on your words," he is saying. "Walk your talk."

Actually, people today are more surprised when someone carries through with an offer or invitation than when someone forgets or lets it slip. We all know words are easy. So when someone does carry through, the effect can be powerful.

Carrying through is costly, of course. Look at what God's love for us cost him. Putting our words into action costs us something too. But it's a wise investment of time and energy. And we don't do it on our own. When we act on the love that God puts into our hearts, God sees to it that the results bring a far bigger payoff in the lives of our neighbors than we could have asked or even imagined (Ephesians 3:20).

—EB

Reflect/Act

- Think about God's promises to you and to others. How many of these promises do you think were just empty words? How faithful has God been in carrying out the good intentions in his heart toward you?
- How can you more faithfully reflect this part of God's nature in your life? Identify any well-meaning offers or invitations you may have made in the past year or the past few months but have not carried out. Ask God how you can follow through on these offers.

Prayer-Starters for Praying 1 John 3:18

Praise God for his absolute and utter faithfulness in carrying out every one of his promises of help and support to you and to your family.

Confess any offers of help or support or friendship that you may have made but have not followed through on.

Thank God for the grace of his offer of forgiveness for all the times when you have fallen short, and for sending Jesus as an unfailing example for you to follow.

Make a list of any recent unfulfilled "good intentions" and commit them to the Lord, *asking* for his help in making the sacrifices required in carrying them out.

Pray a blessing on your neighbors, using 1 John 5:1-5:

Pray that your neighbors may come to believe through your example and witness that Jesus is the Christ, born of God.

Pray that God may open their hearts to love him and to carry out his commands faithfully.

Ask God to help your unsaved neighbors see that his commands are not a burden but that they lead to life and to the ability to love God and others more fully.

Pray that your neighbors may be given the power, through the Spirit's work in their lives, to overcome the world's hold on them and to be true to their word.

DAY 5

Being the Fragrance of Christ

Thanks be to God, who . . . through us spreads everywhere the fragrance of the knowledge of him. For we are to God the aroma of Christ among those who are being saved and those who are perishing. To the one we are the smell of death; to the other, the fragrance of life. And who is equal to such a task?

2 Corinthians 2:14-16

I went to my neighbor's house to return a book last week. When I entered her house, I was enveloped in the aroma of a casserole she had just taken from the oven. The fragrance was welcoming, warm, and inviting. My taste buds began to water, and I realized I was hungry. Before she even said a word, I was wishing for an invitation to dinner.

Aromas can subtly yet powerfully influence our feelings and thoughts. We cannot see or touch odors, but their presence is unmistakable. Perfume makers know the power of a warm, alluring scent. Real-estate agents tell their sellers to sprinkle cinnamon in their ovens and turn the heat on low, to create a warm and homey scent of baking in the home as potential buyers come through.

Did you know there's a spiritual fragrance as well? The love of Christ in the hearts of Christians is a subtle, invisible, yet unmistakable aroma of the Spirit of God. Others may notice it even before you speak to them. They experience it in the acceptance and friendliness of your manner.

What's the source of this fragrance? It comes from spending time with God. It's the love that clings to you when you come from being in God's presence, through prayer and reflection on the Scriptures.

It's the aroma of the Spirit described in 1 Corinthians 13—a patient, kind, selfless nature that "always protects, always trusts, always hopes, always perseveres" (13:7). This loving Spirit within you comes from Jesus, from spending time with him, resting in his love for you, and hearing his words of assurance and instruction in the Bible. This is the aroma your neighbors and the people you work with will notice about you. It's what will attract them to you, encourage them to trust you, and make them want to spend time with you.

As our Scripture passage for this reading points out, some people will not find the fragrance of God's love appealing; instead they will find it displeasing. That's okay—it doesn't mean you are doing something wrong; it just means they are fighting against God's work in their lives. Keep showing them God's love.

When you wear a fragrance, you have to get close enough to people to allow them to smell it. What can you do to get closer to your neighbors—close enough that they can sense the presence of Christ around and within you? Do you share hobbies? Is there a chore you can do for a neighbor who is experiencing illness or hardship? Do you make time to have families over for dessert and conversation? Can you offer to take some of their children with you to the lake or to a good movie? Find ways to spend time and get to know the people God has placed around you—and let them get to know you. You must, as Paul did, open your heart wide to them (2 Corinthians 6:11).

"And who is equal to such a task?" You are, if you take time each day to bathe in the fragrance of God's love. That fragrance will be more compelling and inviting on you than the most expensive perfume.

—EB

Reflect /Act

- What people have shown you the fragrant love of Christ in their lives? What people around you need more of that fragrance in their lives? How can you show it to them?
- Allow yourself space and time each day to seek and experience God's love for you in Christ. How will that experience affect the "aroma" you spread to others who are close to you during the day?

Prayer-Starters for Praying 2 Corinthians 2:14-16

Praise God for the overpowering greatness and sweetness of his love for you and for others.

Confess to God any situations in the past week in which you gave off an aroma different from that of Christ's love, and ask the Spirit to show you how you may need to ask forgiveness of others as well as of God.

Thank God for the wonderful opportunity to share in spreading the aroma of Jesus' love.

Ask God for the time and energy to grow closer to your neighbors and co-workers, and for the wisdom to identify those who will find his love a fragrance that leads to life.

Pray a blessing on your neighbors, using Psalm 138:6-8:

Pray that your neighbors will realize the need to be humble before God, that his love is toward the humble rather than the proud.

Ask God to preserve your neighbors' spiritual and emotional health, even as they "walk in the midst of trouble."

Pray that God's purpose for the life of your neighbors will be fulfilled, and that they may find the aroma of God's love for them in Christ Jesus.

Pray that your neighbors' eyes may be opened to see the love of God that endures forever, and to find the security that God will never abandon them.

Making Time

DAY 1

Mary and Martha

Martha opened her home to [Jesus]. She had a sister called Mary, who sat at the Lord's feet listening to what he said. But Martha was distracted by all the preparations that had to be made. She came to him and asked, "Lord, don't you care that my sister has left me to do the work by myself? Tell her to help me!"

"Martha, Martha," the Lord answered, "you are worried and upset about many things, but only one thing is needed. Mary has chosen what is better . . . ."

Luke 10:38-42

I am a Martha. I work full-time, have three teenagers, coordinate a busy home schedule, am involved in several ministries at church, and try to pursue several personal interests as well. From early morning to late in the evening, I am busy *doing.*

So the story of Mary and Martha is a difficult one for me, because it cuts deep to the heart. Though I am busy doing many good and important things, my busyness gets in the way of listening to and spending time with God and others.

I suspect this is true for many others who work full-time, keep up a home, and contribute to church and community ministries. We live hurried and hectic lives. We can be worried and upset by many things.

"But only one thing is needed," Jesus tells us. *Love God above all, and your neighbor as yourself.* This double-edged command puts our relationship to God and others above achievements, activities, and projects. In the light of this truth, it may be that many busy Christians in North America need to rearrange their priorities.

I once gained a friend at work from a culture and background much different from the one I had grown up in. She and I became prayer partners, and our families occasionally shared meals and outings. One day she called and suggested that we spend a day together the following week.

I looked at my schedule. "I don't know if that will work," I said. "It's pretty busy for the next month or so."

"Edi," she said, "we are friends. Where I come from, that means more than just a ten-minute phone call once a week. It means we take time out just to be with each other."

She was right, of course. I rescheduled "project time" and opened up a day to spend with my friend. We did crafts, went for a walk, prayed together, and just sat around and talked. It was a novel thing for me to take this extended period of time away from my busy schedule, and it enriched our understanding of each other tremendously. It was well worth the time we spent.

The next time you have the opportunity to get to know your neighbor better but you are tempted to pass it up because of your busy schedule, reconsider. Are you, like Martha, "worried and upset about many things"? Jesus told her that "only one thing is needed"—that is, loving our Lord above all so that we can love our neighbor. That's what Mary did.

—EB

Reflect/Act

- How often in the past few months or weeks have you perhaps put a project above a person? What can you do to balance your time spent in activities and your time spent in enjoying God and others?
- As Jesus looks at your daily schedule, will he say you have chosen the one thing that is needed? Identify any changes you think Jesus might suggest in your schedule, and ask him to help you start making those changes this week.

Prayer-Starters for Praying Luke 10:38-42

Praise God for his desire to draw all people into a relationship with himself (1 Timothy 2:3-4).

Confess to God any situations in which your relationship with him and with your neighbors and co-workers has suffered because of your busyness.

Ask God to adjust your perspective on time and priorities to become closer to his perspective. *Ask* him to help you spend time with others, listening and building relationships with them.

Thank God for the opportunities he has already placed in your life to love others as you love yourself—and for the blessings that will come to you and others as you do so.

Pray a BLESSing on those who live or work near you:

Body. Pray that neighbors may be blessed with good health and be free from disease and pain.

Labor. Pray that workaholics, whose lives are dominated by a compulsive "need" to work, may be set free to do "what is needed"—serving Jesus in everything they do.

Emotional. Pray that neighbors will not be distracted from important spiritual pursuits by earthly matters of lesser importance.

Social. Pray that neighbors may have the joy of many good friends and many opportunities to socialize with them.

Spiritual. Pray that unsaved persons will be led by the Holy Spirit to see the need and value of a personal relationship with Jesus Christ.

Entertaining Strangers

Do not forget to entertain strangers, for by so doing some people have entertained angels without knowing it.

Hebrews 13:2

They were standing in a corner, out of everyone's way—a refugee family from Bosnia, though I didn't know it at the time. Someone had invited them to our church, and they had come, hoping to make some connections in this strange new land.

Though the foyer was milling with people, I saw no one stop and speak to this man, his wife, or their three daughters. I walked toward them and heard them speaking to each other in a language other than English. "What if they can't understand me?" I thought. I felt awkward and foolish. But I went to meet them anyway.

When I said hello, the man's face broke into a smile. He introduced his wife and daughters to me, in broken English. The wife could only say, "Hello," but she smiled as warmly as her husband. I found that the daughters, though shy, spoke English fairly well, and we talked briefly before the service. I invited them to sit with our family, and we helped them through the songs and liturgy.

After church, I introduced them to another family and then, mentally taking a quick inventory of my freezer contents, invited everyone to lunch for hot dogs and coleslaw. Not very fancy, but we sat out on the deck and talked about the war in Bosnia, how to find jobs, what schools were best, Dutch and Bosnian recipes, and where to find a better rental house (theirs had cockroaches).

We became firm friends. For two years now our friends from a faraway land have been bringing over their wonderful meat pastries, fresh fish caught on weekend fishing trips, and, best of all, just their happiness to spend time with us. Their loyalty and dedication to our friendship far surpasses any that we have experienced among our North American friends.

We found that we had "entertained angels without knowing it." The point of our Scripture for this reading is that God is watching how we treat his loved ones, especially those in need. (See also Matthew 25:37-40.) Had I allowed our differences and my fear to keep me from approaching these people, we would have missed being a blessing to each other.

People from foreign lands are strangers. But you don't have to look for a refugee family to find a stranger. Who on your street is a stranger to you? Is there someone who has left home and family—whether in Ohio or Mexico or British Columbia—and moved into your neighborhood? Is there an individual or family who keep themselves aloof from neighborhood gatherings—a self-imposed stranger? Is there a lonely widower who has begun to find comfort in alcohol? A refugee family moving into a nearby apartment or taking a new position at work? A newly divorced parent with children?

To open your home to such an individual or family is a wonderful gift that shows God's warm and outreaching love to the stranger. It doesn't take much. Try to keep something in the freezer that you can cook up quickly for last-minute invitations. I have found that our guests are far more interested in a warm invitation and good conversation than the quality of the food served.

Your invitation may open the door of God's family to "the stranger" on your street or at your workplace. What a wonderful way to meet "angels"!

—EB

Reflect/Act

- What makes you hesitate to extend an invitation? Is it fear, awkwardness, over-busyness, lack of resources?
- Identify the last time you invited a stranger into your home. Make plans to invite over someone you don't know very well in the next two weeks, out of hospitality for Jesus' sake.

Prayer-Starters for Praying Hebrews 13:2

Praise God for his openhearted hospitality and generosity to all living things (Psalm 145:15-16).

Confess situations in which you may have placed your needs inappropriately ahead of the needs of a stranger looking for hospitality.

Thank God for the strangers he has placed in your life—on your street or at work—as opportunities to show his loving hospitality.

Ask God for the faith-vision to see that encounters with strangers can turn into blessings.

Pray a blessing on the people around you, using Psalm 145:8-21:

Ask God to pour his grace, rich love, compassion, and goodness into these neighbors' lives, and to be slow to anger about their sins.

Pray that these neighbors will come into contact with someone who will tell them of the glory of God's kingdom and speak of God's mighty acts.

Ask God to lift up neighbors who may have fallen or who may be "down."

Ask the Holy Spirit to be near to these people when they call out to God, that he will hear their cry and save them.

DAY 3

Letting the Children Come

People were bringing little children to Jesus to have him touch them,
but the disciples rebuked them. When Jesus saw this, he was indignant.
He said to them, "Let the little children come to me, and do not hinder
them, for the kingdom of God belongs to such as these."

Mark 10:13-14

Children, of course, bring mud and dirt into the house. They drip juice on the carpet and leave the bathroom sink a mess. They smudge doorways, demand attention, and leave toys on the floor. They might even break the crystal vase your Aunt Jennie gave you.

There are many good reasons not to let neighborhood children into your home.

There's also a good reason to let them come: *Jesus has asked them to.*

Whether you have children or not, whether you are old, young, or middle-aged, there may be children in your neighborhood who need a stable father figure, some gentle mothering, or a substitute grandparent they can confide in.

Even more, they need to know Jesus, who lives in your home. If your home is not open to them, how will they meet Jesus?

It doesn't take much to open your home. Children require little more than love, a glass of juice, a cookie, and a listening ear. In each of these, even in the smallest of acts—a cup of cold water—you are sending out small tendrils of loving concern through which Jesus can make himself known to the children in your neighborhood.

You could keep on hand some puzzles, coloring books, markers, or simple toys for younger children. Introduce yourself to their parents, who will need to know you before they feel comfortable with their children stopping by your house.

For older children, find odd jobs for them to do, and pay them well. Most adolescents have a deep need to be useful to someone, and often they are not given the invitation. Children take in a lot. They know love when they see it. Can you find Jesus' love in your heart for the child who may otherwise seem like a nuisance?

Getting to know the children who live around you will open up opportunities to invite them to special children's activities at your church—and perhaps, through them, you can draw in the rest of the family to know Jesus, if they don't know him and serve him already. Or you may simply be able to provide a stable, loving, adult presence that someday may give helpful advice or encouragement that will play a crucial role in these children's lives.

You may be too busy with adult concerns, or you may value your home and possessions too highly to feel glad about inviting children into your home. But give these suggestions some serious thought. Don't make the same mistake as Jesus' disciples did. "Let the little children come," for "the kingdom of heaven belongs to such as these."

—EB

Reflect/Act

- Besides your parents, what grownups do you remember being important in your life as a child? Why were they special to you?
- Ask God to show you what you can do to make more of an impact on the lives of children who live around you. Give at least one child in your neighborhood a kind and positive word, either verbally or in a written note, that praises them for a good quality.

Prayer-Starters for Praying Mark 10:13-14

Praise Jesus Christ, who opened his arms to children even when adults were pressing in around him, and in doing so taught a powerful lesson about the kingdom of heaven.

If you have been impatient with a child recently, due to your own busyness or preoccupation, *confess* that impatience now and ask forgiveness.

Thank God for the blessings he intended children to be in your life and for the lessons you can learn from them.

Ask for opportunities to develop good friendships with children and for sensitivity in relating to children.

Pray a BLESSing on the children who live near you:

Body. Pray that God will keep these children safe from physical danger, and thank him for the angels he provides for their safety (Matthew 18:10).

Labor. Ask God for safe learning environments at school and for parents to teach good values, skills, and habits to their children.

Emotional. Pray that these children's needs for a loving, stable home environment may be met (Ephesians 6:1-4).

Social. Ask God for a circle of friends and supportive, Christian adult role models in the lives of these children.

Spiritual. Pray that these children will hear the truth about God and will be able to find it, like a hidden treasure, and understand the fear of God (Proverbs 2:1-5).

DAY 4

Being a Good Samaritan

"A man . . . fell into the hands of robbers. They stripped him of his clothes, beat him and went away, leaving him half dead. A priest happened to be going down the same road, and when he saw the man, he passed by on the other side. . . . But a Samaritan . . . took pity on him. He went to him and bandaged his wounds, pouring on oil and wine. Then he put the man on his own donkey, took him to an inn, and took care of him."

Luke 10:30-34

Jesus tells of a Samaritan—not a "religious" person—who stops to help someone bleeding by the side of the road. This story, of course, is a little removed from our own experience. We don't often see people lying beaten and unconscious on the roadside. At least not physically. But what about those who are beaten up by loss of employment, divorce, drug addiction, depression, or something else? How easy is it to walk by and pretend we don't see, like the "religious" person in Jesus' story?

The priest walked by because the need was so great, and he probably had other (and important) things to do. How could he possibly cope with this man's problems? The man was almost dead! It would take all of the priest's time, and much of his money, to help. He had every excuse to walk by. Besides, he may have had commitments with others whom he didn't want to disappoint.

We also have every excuse to walk by someone who has been badly hurt by life, or by addiction, or by broken relationships. What if it takes a lot of time? What if we have to give a lot of ourselves in order to be a neighbor to this person in need? What about the other important things we have to do?

Yet Jesus holds up the Samaritan as the one who was a true neighbor. "Love your neighbor as yourself" is the command that is second only to loving God (Matthew 22:39).

How can you love your neighbor as God wants you to? First, spend time in prayer. Ask God to show you people whom he has put into your life and who may be feeling beaten, or near to spiritual death, by the struggles they face. Ask God to show you whom you might be closing your eyes to, and whom he may want you to help. (Remember, God does not ask you to help him save the whole world. One co-worker, one family, one neighbor—that's a start.)

How can you help? Start with a kind word, a smile, a question about how things are going. Get to know a person well enough to know what support is needed. Then ask God to provide that support—through you, if he wishes, or through some other channel. Let that person know you are praying for him or her in regard to his or her need.

Write a note of encouragement—not just once, but regularly. Maintain phone contact, if possible, just to keep in touch. Include the person or family in some of your own family's activities.

Remember that in all of this God is the one paying the bills, not you. God will provide you with the time needed, the wisdom to deal with problems, the love you are called to show. It is God's riches, not your own, that you are passing on to your neighbor.

—EB

Reflect/Act

- Which of the people in Jesus' story can you most identify with? Have you ever been "beaten up" and in need of help? Have you ever passed by someone who was? Have you ever stopped to help? What happened?
- On a piece of paper write down the name of a person whom you sense God is asking you to be a neighbor to. Carry that paper with you wherever you go, to remind you to pray throughout the day for that person.

Prayer-Starters for Praying Luke 10:30-34

Praise God that he has been a "good neighbor" to you, giving his life so that you could be saved and find new life in him.

Confess a situation in which you may have walked by someone in great need or distress and looked the other way.

Thank God for his ability to help you overcome the desire not to "get involved," and for his compassionate love that's ready to flow through you to others.

Ask God to show you whom he may be asking you to help.

Pray a BLESSing on your neighbors and co-workers:

Body. Pray for neighbors and co-workers who are weakened and discouraged by long-term illnesses or disabilities, that God will be their strength and will provide encouragement through you and others.

Labor. Pray for those who do not have a job and have been frustrated in their attempts to find one, that God will provide them with work that uses their gifts.

Emotional. Pray for emotional strength for parents who are going through troubled times with their children, or spouses who are bearing a heavy load of marital conflict or unhappiness.

Social. Pray for a supportive group of people with whom your neighbors or co-workers can share some of their burdens (Galatians 6:2).

Spiritual. Pray that God will use your neighbors' or co-workers' time of need to open their hearts to his leading in their lives.

DAY 5

Who Cares?

An expert in the law . . . . asked Jesus, "And who is my neighbor?"
In reply Jesus said: "A man was going down from Jerusalem to
Jericho, when he fell into the hands of robbers. They stripped him of his
clothes, beat him and went away, leaving him half dead."

Luke 10:25-30

To answer the question of an "expert" who was testing him, Jesus began by portraying a person in a hopeless condition—stripped, beaten, robbed, and left for dead. The picture represents more than a single man. It's really a picture of our world—all the broken, hurting, depraved persons in our sin-ravaged world.

We live in an incredibly hurting world. Surveys tell us that 40,000 children die of starvation each day; 800 million people are destitute; and 10 million are refugees with no place to call home. In the United States 13.5 million people are physically disabled; 7 million are mentally disabled; 7 million are alcoholics; and half a million are in prison. Add to this the physically abused, sexually abused, battered spouses, victims of crime, the incurably ill, the permanently injured, desperate teenagers, lonely and forgotten senior citizens—and it all adds up to a deeply hurting world. This is the world we live in. We travel the road that passes by these hurting ones.

The pressing question is *Who cares?* Who cares when my neighbor, your neighbor, hurts?

Jesus does! The good Samaritan, who stopped, treated the suffering man, loved and lifted him, and paid the price for his care, was none other than Jesus Christ and all who have faithfully carried his name throughout the centuries. He who invites all people to cast their cares on him and promises, "I will give you rest" (Matthew 11:28), declares, "Anyone who has faith in me will do what I have been doing" (John 14:12). That means you and I, as his followers, will do the works our Lord has done.

So who cares? Jesus does, and so do all who love and serve him. He calls us to be neighbors to hurting ones who are ravaged by the miseries of life.

To the "expert" who, in the end, correctly identified the true neighbor as "the one who showed mercy," Jesus says, "Go and do likewise" (Luke 10:37). To you and me he says the same.

Look around! Do you see the hurting ones along all the roads you travel? They are there. Let's not pass them by.

—AVG

Reflect/Act

• Write down the names of several hurting persons you know. Perhaps they live right on your street. Try to imagine what life is like for them. Try to connect with them in some way to learn more about their true condition.

Prayer-Starters for Praying Luke 10:25-30

Give *thanks* that in all the hurts and sorrows of life Jesus never passes us by. If you have been neglectful of hurting persons around you, *confess* that sin to the Lord.

Ask God to open your eyes and your heart to hurting persons and to give you the compassion that Christ has for them.

Pray a BLESSing on your hurting neighbors:

Body. Pray for the physically handicapped, physically abused, battered spouses, incurably ill, and people who are malnourished or dying of starvation.

Labor. Pray for refugees, for the destitute, and for the chronically unemployed.

Emotional. Pray for those who are emotionally scarred, depressed, discouraged, and anxious.

Social. Pray for desperate teenagers, lonely and forgotten older persons, and people who are socially outcast.

Spiritual. Pray for those who are spiritually blind and in bondage to Satan.

A SUGGESTION FOR MINISTRY ACTIVITY

Connecting with Neighbors

Caring involves being present, making connections with people in their own daily lives. Sometimes connecting happens naturally. Sometimes we need to be intentional to make it happen. Here are some ways in which *Light-House* members can easily connect with neighbors:

- Prayerwalk your neighborhood, looking for people to meet.
- Organize a block party.
- Initiate a neighborhood-wide garage sale.
- Volunteer as a "neighborhood watch" house.
- Initiate car pools for school or work.
- Invite neighbors over for a Christmas-carol sing.
- Volunteer to work on a voter-registration drive.
- Plan a Halloween giveaway.
- Meet neighborhood parents at athletic events involving their kids.
- Make an effort to meet apartment-complex neighbors at common areas such as the pool, laundry room, mailbox, and so on.
- Inform people of your profession or trade and make yourself available if they might need the kind of help you offer.
- Look for neighbors at school functions, town meetings, ball games, and so on.

Reaching the Outsider

DAY 1

Loving the Stranger

The Lord your God . . . . defends the cause of the fatherless and the widow, and loves the alien, giving him food and clothing. And you are to love those who are aliens, for you yourselves were aliens . . . .
Deuteronomy 10:17-19

"Never talk to strangers!" This warning echoes through many homes and schools in North America. We want our children to be on their guard against people they don't know. So we say, "Don't trust them! Don't talk to them! Don't go with them!"

There are reasons for this caution, of course. And I understand them; my own childhood was harmed by a stranger. The unknown always brings with it the possibility of danger. But, as Christians, we have to ask, *What perspective, what frame of reference, are we operating under?* Do we open our hearts and homes only to those who are familiar to us?

Old Testament hospitality was almost completely different. In the nomadic, wandering culture that Abraham grew up in, it was expected that one would invite a stranger traveling by to stop for a meal and a night's lodging. God wanted his people, the Israelites, to be outstanding in this respect. They were to represent God's own outreaching heart for the stranger, the hungry one, the "alien." Hospitality to the "alien" was commanded and expected.

"Aliens" were people from other countries. That meant they came from different cultures, value systems, and religions. They also spoke different languages. The very word *alien* means "other, different, strange." Families in Israel were to provide food, shelter, and clothing for these people and to show them the hospitality of God himself.

In my travels abroad as a student and later as an adult, I have been surprised to find hospitality in many different countries. I found that Germans, English, Irish, Austrians, Hungarians, and citizens of Turkey would converse with me, ask questions, and invite me into their home—even when they spoke only broken English. They would feed me and send me away with gifts: a little vase, a shawl, a bar of chocolate. Those are the warmest memories of my travels. Hospitality makes a powerful impression on a stranger.

Do you know people living or working near you whose culture is completely different from yours? People who perhaps speak only broken English? Who are struggling to make sense of the culture around them?

Do you know another kind of "alien"—someone who is different, strange, an outsider? Perhaps it's someone who does not dress as you do, or share the same value system, or believe in God, or use the same religious language. Maybe it's someone who is different enough (perhaps because of mental limitations or physical appearance or economic status) not to fit in with the culture you are comfortable in. How can you open your home and your world to someone like that?

There are risks in doing so, of course. But there may be greater risks in not doing so: the risk of losing the opportunity to draw someone into the family of God.

—EB

Reflect/Act

- Have you ever traveled to a different place and been surprised by the kindness or hospitality of a stranger? How did that make you feel?
- Think of all the people you know who are from a culture or background that's not the same as yours. Plan to introduce yourself to one of them and get to know him or her a little better this week.

Prayer-Starters for Praying Deuteronomy 10:17-19

Praise God for his openhearted welcome to all who are without a close-knit family and for all who are "strangers" who don't fit in.

Confess your feelings of hesitation or inadequacy in befriending people who are different from you.

Ask God to allow you to participate in his care and love for the "alien."

Thank God for drawing you close to him when you were a stranger—even an enemy!—to him (see Romans 5:10).

Pray a BLESSing on the strangers who live and work near you:

Body. Ask God to provide for any financial needs these neighbors might have—for food, shelter, clothing—through you, if he wishes (1 John 3:16-18).

Labor. Pray for adequate work and income to meet those needs.

Emotional. Ask God to provide hospitable, loving people to open their homes to these neighbors, to help fill the place of friends and family they may have left behind.

Social. Pray for a network of supportive friends and neighbors.

Spiritual. Ask God to bring these neighbors into his family, where love is given and shared freely (1 John 4:7).

DAY 2

"I Was Hungry"

"Then the King will say to those on his right, 'Come, you who are blessed by my Father; take your inheritance, the kingdom prepared for you since the creation of the world. For I was hungry and you gave me something to eat, I was thirsty and you gave me something to drink, I was a stranger and you invited me in . . . ."

Matthew 25:34-35

When I was growing up, I didn't know anyone who was hungry. My friends all belonged to well-fed, second-generation immigrant families who served steaming pots of soup or big roasts or loaves of fresh bread and rolls. There was always enough to go around, even in our relatively poor family of ten people. All our dinner guests appeared well fed and left our table even more so.

Things have not changed much since then. Today I still greet well-fed neighbors and co-workers. In fact, most of us battle a weight problem. The only hungry people I know personally are dieters.

Our family does give regularly to famine relief and to our church's food pantry and to the city mission kitchen. So we do, in a sense, feed the hungry. If you wish to do this more personally but you are unsure how to go about it, call a local service agency or your community kitchen and ask how you can become involved. This is certainly part of what the King meant when he said, "I was hungry and you gave me something to eat."

But not all hunger is physical. The word *hunger* connotes an unfulfilled desire, a yearning or craving; it means that something is lacking. *Thirst* implies the same, adding the quality of dryness, of desperate need for water.

In the life of anyone who is separated from God, there's an unfulfilled craving. There's a dryness, a yearning for something that is lacking. People you live nearby or work with may be trying to fill that craving with money or things or drugs or social status or power.

But this yearning is a hunger and thirst that only Jesus can fill. He alone can say, "I am the bread of life" (John 6:35), and, "I am the living water" (see John 4:10). You and I are called to offer people that bread and water, to bring the good news that their hunger can be filled only by Jesus.

Yet we might hesitate to approach such people. They may intimidate us, or we might just plain dislike them or find their way of life impossible to understand.

But the King will say, "*I* was hungry"; "*I* was thirsty." God has such passion for these people that he puts himself in their place. It's as if God himself were sitting in that house across the street, waiting for a kind word, some friendly comfort, and the good news that there is hope, joy, and peace to be found in Jesus—even in this sad, often empty world.

What would happen if you offered forgiveness to the co-worker who has so often offended you? If you brought a jar of soup and a vase of flowers from your yard over to the elderly man whose children seldom visit? If you opened your kitchen and your heart to the woman who is going through a divorce? You would be offering the love of Jesus to people who may be hungry and thirsty for him.

—EB

Reflect/Act

- What things in life have you been hungry for besides food? When have you felt spiritually or emotionally thirsty?
- Think of three concrete ways in which you can offer Jesus' love to those who are hungry and thirsty during this coming week. Ask God to help you follow up on your ideas.

Prayer-Starters for Praying Matthew 25:34-35

Praise God for the kingdom and inheritance he has prepared for you since the creation of the world.

Confess that there have been times when you haven't recognized God in the people around you who were hungry and thirsty for physical or spiritual nourishment.

Ask for the grace to be able to see Jesus in needy situations.

Pray a blessing on your neighbors, using Psalm 63:1-5:

Pray that your neighbors will see that God is the only One who can quench their spiritual thirst; pray also that they will earnestly seek him.

Pray that your neighbors will be drawn to worship in a church in which they will behold God's power and glory.

Pray that these neighbors will experience God's love, which is "better than life."

Pray that their souls' hunger will be filled with Jesus, the bread of life, so that they will be "satisfied as with the richest of foods."

DAY 3

Being Wise Toward Outsiders

Be wise in the way you act toward outsiders; make the most of every opportunity. Let your conversation be always full of grace, seasoned with salt, so that you may know how to answer everyone.

Colossians 4:5-6

There are two people I've gotten to know better than almost anyone besides my immediate family and my prayer group. One is a woman at work, and one is a neighbor who lives two doors down. One is a Christian, and one is not.

The reason I've gotten to know them so well is that both are my walking partners. With one I walk once a week on my lunch hour; with the other I walk on weekends or summer evenings. We put on our old walking shoes, wear a jacket in cool weather, and spend about an hour stretching our legs—and talking with each other.

These weekly conversations have opened windows for us into each other's lives. I have been able to share my faith, as well as the daily enjoyments and frustrations of life. I have had ample opportunity to let my conversation be "full of grace, seasoned with salt," to my neighbor who is outside the church, as well as to my sister in Christ at work.

Conversations with both of these friends are a pleasure and an encouragement to me. With my neighbor I talk about many things: gardening, crime prevention efforts in our neighborhood, our struggles with parenting teenage children, neighbors whose son is dying of AIDS, the difficult divorce of a mutual friend, and sometimes even the frequent hypocrisy and close-mindedness of "religious" people.

I also pray especially before walking with her—perhaps because I know that ultimately so much is at stake. I pray that God will accompany us with his Spirit and will give me wisdom as I talk.

I have prayed that my neighbor will ask questions that provide an opening for me to share what I've learned about God through the Bible and through my own life as a Christian. I pray that I will not be afraid to have "salty" conversation—in other words, to say things that are distinctly different from the way the rest of the world looks at life.

Sometimes I feel a bit inadequate in this. What if my neighbor's knowledge of the Christian faith is based entirely on her acquaintance with me? I remember the apostle Paul's words: "Who is equal to such a task?" (2 Corinthians 2:16).

But I also remember Paul's encouragement from the same passage: "But thanks be to God, who always leads us in triumphal procession in Christ and through us spreads everywhere the fragrance of the knowledge of him" (2 Corinthians 2:14). It's comforting to know that God has chosen weak and flawed believers like me to be salt and light to unbelievers, and that he provides what is needed for such work.

The verses from Colossians 4 above assume, of course, that there will be opportunities for conversation between you and "outsiders." Have you made time in your life for such opportunities? Are you willing to do so? You may be the only salt and light that they come into contact with.

—EB

Reflect/Act
- Why is it important to be careful in your conversations with outsiders?
- In what areas of your life do you have close personal contact with an outsider? Think of at least two ways in which you can increase that contact in the coming week.

Prayer-Starters for Praying Colossians 4:5-6

Praise God for his ability to impart wisdom to believers through the Holy Spirit.

Confess that in conversations with unbelievers you may have been unwise in what you said or you may have missed an opportunity to share the good news of Jesus.

Thank God for calling you to act as a seasoning and as a preservative in this world.

Ask God to fill you with his grace and give you opportunities to speak with outsiders.

Pray a blessing for your neighbors, using Romans 10:14-17:

Pray that God will send people into your neighbors' lives to speak the good news to them, if they don't have a relationship with Jesus.

Pray that when your neighbors hear the good news about Jesus, they will believe and commit their lives to him.

Pray that this faith will change their lives so that they, in turn, may bring the good news to others.

DAY 4

Kindness to the Poor

He who is kind to the poor lends to the Lord,
and he will reward him for what he has done.

Proverbs 19:17

A friend of my parents, someone who had accumulated much wealth, was often approached by people who were in financial trouble. I don't know how much he opened his wallet in those circumstances, but I do remember his comment one evening over coffee. "You have to be careful with those people," he told us children. "Sometimes they can't pay you back. In those cases, it would probably be better never to lend them anything in the first place. It just makes for bad feelings."

I thought that made sense at the time.

But then we had a neighbor whose father got sick with hepatitis and couldn't work to pay his children's school tuition. We helped them out financially, without expecting to get anything back. My dad didn't let them know the money was from us; he would put it in a blank envelope and place it in their mailbox at night.

Our aunt needed eye surgery that insurance wouldn't cover. We collected our dollars and gave her enough to be able to go ahead with the surgery.

At work we gathered food and kitchen goods for a fellow employee who was struck with a long-term illness and had to live on a small disability check. We also donated unused vacation hours into her account to ensure that she would receive pay during her time off.

A few streets away we met a family with young children who moved here from another country. The mother is going to school, and the father is trying to support the family with odd jobs. We slip extra money into their mail slot every now and then to help with their grocery bill.

In each of these instances, we gave without thinking about getting our money back. Someone we cared about was in need, and it was a joy to help, even when we didn't have much ourselves. We were giving money away, but we were also lending to the Lord.

If you think about that, it's a mind-boggling idea that we can lend to the Lord, who is essentially the Chief Financial Officer of the universe. Every penny in my wallet got there by God's grace—but once I give it away to the poor, God

110

treats it as a loan to himself and makes sure that one day I will be repaid—and with abundance besides (Luke 6:38).

Look around your neighborhood or workplace. Where is there an opportunity for you to lend to the Lord? Don't be afraid to do so. In the long run, it will yield a great deal more interest than the going market rates—both in the lives of the people you help and in your own life.

—EB

Reflect/Act

- Read 2 Corinthians 9:6-15. What happens when a person obeys the prompting of God's Spirit to share his or her wealth?
- Give thanks that God has given you enough to give something away. Identify one person whom you feel God is asking you to encourage and uplift with a small (or large) financial gift or other material support, and make plans to do so this week.

Prayer-Starters for Praying Proverbs 19:17

Praise God, who has created and owns this world and all the wealth in it (Job 38:4-7).

Confess if you have not been sensitive at times to the Spirit's prompting to give to someone in need, or if you have given in to the temptation to keep your wealth for yourself.

Thank God for his ability to give you all you need for every good work.

Commit yourself "to be rich in good deeds, to be generous and willing to share" (1 Timothy 6:18).

Pray a blessing on your neighbors and co-workers in need, using Matthew 6:25-33:

Pray that God will provide for the basic needs of your neighbors and co-workers, just as he provides for the birds of the air and the grass of the field.

Pray that these neighbors and co-workers will become aware of how deeply God is concerned for all their needs.

Ask God to turn their hearts to seek first his kingdom and righteousness and to know that God will give them all the other things they need as well.

Ask God to show you the ways in which he may be asking you to help provide for someone in need.

The Need to Be Needed

When a Samaritan woman came to draw water, Jesus said to her, "Will you give me a drink?"

John 4:7

It was a huge cabin cruiser, not something you'd ever think of building in a backyard. But my friend did it. It was about thirty feet long, complete with a comfortable cabin and a huge engine. It took him three years to build it, and having virtually no mechanical ability myself, I was overwhelmed.

"How did you do it?" I asked. "Did you really figure out everything yourself? Didn't you have any plans?"

"No," my pastor friend replied, "I didn't have any plans, and I figured it all out by myself. Except, that is, for one thing. I could not figure out how to drill that long hole through the beam for the propeller shaft. That was too much."

Then he told me a fascinating story connected with that problem. God used it to bring a very difficult character into his family.

"I had witnessed to one of my neighbors many times, but whatever I would say about Christianity fell on totally deaf ears. This fellow was just not interested. And there was no way I could reach out to him. He was proudly independent. He had been a carpenter all his life—a very skilled carpenter."

"When I tried to figure out how to get that hole drilled, the Lord put his name into my mind. I realized at that moment that maybe my neighbor's greatest need was to be needed! I could ask him if he knew how to drill that long hole for my propeller shaft."

"Wow, what a breakthrough! All the hard shell in my neighbor's character dropped away when I put myself in a position of needing his services. I offered to pay for his time, of course, but my request to him drew him into my project, and over the next few months we were drawn into a deep friendship. It was that friendship that opened the door of his heart. Since I had dignified him and in that way met his need of being needed, he was profoundly grateful and listened as I shared the message of the Savior with him. He became a faithful and active member of the church."

This was the same approach Jesus used when he met the Samaritan woman at the well. He recognized that her greatest need was the need to be needed, the need for dignity. He met that need when he asked her for a drink of water. And she was surprised! She could hardly believe that a man, a Jewish man, would ask a favor of a woman, especially a Samaritan woman. Jesus dignified her by asking her to help him.

When we think of caring, we almost immediately think of people who need something, and then we give them something even though they might really need the opposite. To really care for people means that we sensitively look for something they have to offer; it means we try to fill their "need to be needed" by asking for a favor that we know a person can do and that this person enjoys doing.

When you ask God to show you how to care, be certain not just to look at what you might give to your neighbor. Also ask God to show you how to dignify your neighbor by allowing him or her to give to you.

—JDV

Reflect/Act

- Think of some specific ways in which others could help you.
- Intentionally ask for help today. It could be something very small. Be alert to how you feel in asking and how the other person responds.

Prayer-Starters for Praying John 4:7

Thank God that he has dignified you with important things to do for him.
Confess if at times you have not recognized the need of others to be needed.
Ask God to help you dignify others with appropriate requests for help.

Pray a BLESSing on your neighbors and fellow employees:

Body. Pray that your neighbors and co-workers may keep their bodies fit as temples of the Holy Spirit (1 Corinthians 6:19).

Labor. Pray that God will give these neighbors many opportunities to make use of the skills and talents he has given them.

Emotional. Pray for those who feel useless because they have not found their niche in life or have not found a way to use their skills and talents meaningfully.

Social. Ask the Lord to provide meaningful friends and relationships for those who are lonely.

Spiritual. Pray that your neighbors and fellow employees may come to know their true worth in God's eyes and may be drawn to him.

Breaking Down Walls

Loving Your Enemy

"You have heard that it was said, 'Love your neighbor and hate your enemy.' But I tell you: Love your enemies and pray for those who persecute you, that you may be sons of your Father in heaven. He causes his sun to rise on the evil and the good, and sends rain on the righteous and the unrighteous. If you love those who love you, what reward will you get?"
Matthew 5:43-46

I have to admit that my co-worker and I have a hard time getting along. She and I have very different personalities, and we find it difficult to understand each other. On some issues at the office, we find ourselves as opponents, not colleagues. Some unkind words have been said, and as a result there is friction. Though we are outwardly polite, underneath is often a feeling of tension.

This situation has not been easy for me to deal with. Daily contact with a person who has sometimes treated me unfairly (in my estimation) and has spoken ill of me to others is not pleasant. From time to time we have attempted to talk things out, but so far that has only worsened the situation.

For a while resentment built up in my heart. Though outwardly polite, I inwardly nurtured a dislike of my co-worker and daily reviewed a list of grievances. Though I prayed for my co-worker and myself, I was at a loss for what to do. Should I be aggressive and accusing? Should I stuff down my feelings and pretend everything was okay?

Then I read this: "The Lord's servant must not quarrel; instead, he must be kind to everyone, able to teach, not resentful. Those who oppose him he must gently instruct, in the hope that God will grant them repentance leading to a knowledge of the truth" (2 Timothy 2:24-25).

Those words leaped off the page. I instantly prayed, "Lord, take away my resentful heart. Teach me how to instruct gently, without anger or condescension. Use me in any way you wish to lead my co-worker to a knowledge of the truth that you are real and that you love her."

God answered that prayer quickly. He somehow took the sting of resentment from within my heart (what a miracle the working of the Spirit is!). Nothing has changed in the way my co-worker treats me, but I have a spirit of love and gentleness that was not there before. I no longer feel threatened by my co-worker; instead I have a sense of expectation that God will continue to work in both her and me.

I am waiting for the Spirit's opportunity and prompting, and I continue to pray for peace in our relationship. I am looking for ways to care for her.

God has a plan for his people: to show that he loves all people, even the unjust and the unkind. In order to be mirror images of God, we are to love our enemies and pray for those who persecute us. For a graphic example of this kind of love, simply look at Jesus on the cross.

Who in your life has become an irritant, an opponent, someone who seems to be out to get you? Have you asked God to send his sunshine into that person's life? Have you asked God to pour his love into your heart? When you do this, miracles begin to happen.

—EB

Reflect/Act

- Is it fair of God to ask that you love your enemy? Why or why not?
- Let God bring to mind someone who has hurt you, someone whom you now regard as an enemy. How might it be possible to love someone who has slandered and worked against you? What would you need in order to be able to do this? Ask God to show you one thing you can do this week to show love to your enemy.

Prayer-Starters for Praying Matthew 5:43-46

Praise God for his lovingkindness, which is poured out on believers and unbelievers alike.

Ask God to show you any times when your love and kindness may have been limited to those who have been loving toward you. *Confess* those shortcomings, and seek God's forgiveness, remembering also to forgive others who have wronged you (Matthew 6:14-15).

Thank Jesus for the example he gave of loving his enemies, and commit yourself to following his example.

Pray a BLESSing on your neighbors and co-workers:

Body. Pray that God will provide your neighbors and co-workers with the basic needs for living (Matthew 6:31-32).

Labor. Ask God to bless their efforts at work and to prosper the use of their gifts and talents.

Emotional. Ask God to fill any emotional needs through the Holy Spirit so that these neighbors may be filled with the Lord's lovingkindness.

Social. Ask God to use your relationships with your neighbors and co-workers to reflect his amazing, abundant, and forgiving love.

Spiritual. Pray that these persons may grow by God's Spirit to show true humility, selflessness, and love (Philippians 2:2-4).

DAY 2

Payback Time

*Make sure that nobody pays back wrong for wrong, but always try to be
kind to each other and to everyone else.*

1 Thessalonians 5:15

From down the street, another neighbor who attends my church came to me
with a problem. His nextdoor neighbor, a very particular gardener, had taken
the liberty of trimming some of his prized apple trees, because they were shading her flower garden. She had cut them back well over the property line.

"And," he said, "she did it all without asking. Just piled the branches up by
the curb, without even saying anything about it. I can't believe it!"

His voice was restrained, but I could hear the anger underneath. "Did you talk
to her about it?" I asked.

"Yes, but she just said she was sorry if I was offended by it, but she didn't
think I would miss a few small branches that had been shading her day lilies.
And that was it!"

He stood for a moment, thinking. "I want to ask you something," he said.
"She asked me last week if she could use the other half of my double garage to
park in this winter, because we have only one car now, with the kids gone. I
said we'd consider it. Now I feel like telling her to forget it totally! What would
you do? I just get so steamed, I can't think straight about it."

My friend's reaction was natural and human. Our first response when someone wrongs us is a desire to wrong them back. Yet, from Jesus' sermon in
Matthew 5 to the closing words of the epistles, it's clear that God wants us to
do something entirely opposite. "I tell you: Love your enemies and pray for
those who persecute you," Jesus taught (Matthew 5:44). And "do not repay
anyone evil for evil," wrote Paul (Romans 12:17).

There's a good reason for this. Paul puts it this way: "Do not be overcome by
evil, but overcome evil with good" (Romans 12:21). If my friend retaliates
against his neighbor by refusing her garage space (which he has every human
right to do), he will have been overcome by evil. But God is asking him to
overcome evil with good.

Is there a neighbor or co-worker with whom you have been having a conflict?
Have you felt that you have every right, humanly speaking, to pay back that
person evil for evil?

God is asking you to do something else. God's way is a complete turnaround from the way our human nature thinks and acts. God wants us to leave the issue of justice with him, and instead to care for any neighbor who offends us, to overcome that person's evil with good.

This may mean giving a sincere compliment to a co-worker on something that is honestly praiseworthy. Or perhaps you can offer to help with a neighbor's chore, or share an abundance of produce or a good, fresh strawberry pie. God is asking you to go out of your way to do good to persons who offend, so that the evil they have been trapped in can be overcome by God's goodness.

How else will they see God, except in the unexpectedness of finding his love in you?

—EB

Reflect/Act

- What would have been your response to the woman who cut back her neighbor's fruit trees? What would have been Jesus' response?
- Think of a situation in which you can pay back good for evil this week. Ask God to use that opportunity to teach someone about his love and kindness.

Prayer-Starters for Praying 1 Thessalonians 5:15

Praise God for his wisdom and power, which go far beyond ours, especially in matters of justice and vengeance.

Ask God to show you any times when you may have taken revenge into your own hands instead of acting kindly toward someone who has wronged you.

Confess your own wrongdoing and ask God to help you forgive your neighbor, just as you have been forgiven (Matthew 6:14-15).

Commit to God those situations in which you have been hurt or wronged, and give up to God any desire you may have for revenge (Romans 12:19).

Pray a blessing on your neighbors, using Philippians 2:1-4:

Ask God to draw your neighbors into a fellowship of believers in which they will find unity in Christ and comfort in his love.

Ask God to restore like-mindedness and respect to relationships that are strained or broken among your neighbors.

Pray that any spirit of ambition and pride at work in your neighbors' lives will be defeated and replaced with Christ's humility.

Ask God to deeply influence your neighbors' lives through the actions of people who selflessly look out for others' interests.

DAY 3

Peaceable People

*Be ready to do whatever is good, to slander no one, to be peaceable
and considerate, and to show true humility toward all men.*

Titus 3:1-2

Gossip is a danger *everywhere.* Some neighborhoods and workplaces may be
worse for gossip than other places, but wherever people talk about others, the
potential for gossip is there.

A well-meaning neighbor, for example, meets me on the street and shares
what was meant to be confidential information given her by another neighbor
about her potential divorce. By way of "caring" for another person, an office
worker mentions the struggles that person is having with her teenage children.

I might question why a man's car is parked so often outside my next-door
neighbor's house when her husband is at work. Or my husband might remark
that the couple across the street often seem a little disoriented and "high."

When we are neighbors or co-workers, we will sooner or later learn the intimate weaknesses and failings of the people we live near and work with. And
our great adversary, the devil, tempts us (often without much resistance) to pass
along "juicy" tidbits to others, even under the guise of a caring attitude.

God, however, seeks to use such opportunities to reveal his character in you:
"Be ready to do whatever is good, to slander no one . . . ." The first way you
can care for your neighbor in this kind of situation is to keep your neighbor's
confidence and not pass on "juicy" information.

And if you are hearing someone else do so, you might say, "I'd rather not
hear that; it sounds like confidential information that I'd rather not know." This
is a gentle rebuke that will help others think about what they are sharing. It's
also a way of being peaceable and considerate toward those who are being
talked about.

But there's more. God allows us to learn about others' weaknesses and struggles so that we can bring his goodness and healing power to bear in their lives.
If you have become aware of a neighbor's or a co-worker's struggles or flaws,
get on your knees and pray for that person. That should be your first response,
always.

Then ask God to show you how he may want to use you in that situation.
Your participation may be limited simply to prayer, or God may give you the

opportunity to ask your neighbor how things are going, to offer a word of encouragement, to let that person know you are interested and willing to listen.

And don't forget about "showing true humility" toward everyone. Remember that you have weaknesses and failings and are made of the same stuff as your neighbor or co-worker. Your own life could be the subject of other people's slander.

So leave gossip alone. Instead, reach out in love to the person who may be struggling with family problems or personal sins. In doing so, you will be following Jesus and showing his love.

—EB

Reflect/Act

- Have you ever been hurt by another person's gossip about you? How did that feel?
- Think of one person whose weaknesses or struggles you have discovered lately. Commit to praying for that person instead of talking about him or her, as well as offering verbal encouragement, if possible.

Prayer-Starters for Praying Titus 3:1-2

Praise Jesus for his example of speaking the truth in love at all times.

Confess that at times your conversation about others has not been motivated by a desire to do what is good, peaceable, and considerate.

Thank God for his forgiveness, and *ask* God to teach you true humility as you speak about others.

Pray a blessing on your neighbors and co-workers, using 2 Thessalonians 3:1-5:

Pray that these neighbors may hear the message of the Lord and honor it in their hearts.

Pray that God will deliver them from the evil intentions of others.

Ask God to strengthen your neighbors and co-workers when they are tempted or attacked by the evil one.

Ask God to direct their hearts "into God's love" and into Christ's patient and persistent call on their lives.

Breaking the Dividing Wall

Now in Christ Jesus you who once were far away have been brought near through the blood of Christ. For he himself is our peace, who has made the two one and has destroyed the barrier, the dividing wall of hostility.

Ephesians 2:13-14 (see also verses 11-18)

"Why has no one been over to see me?" The angry voice on the phone belonged to Olivia, an elderly African American woman who lived across the street. "Don't people know I am sick?"

Olivia *was* quite sick—diagnosed with cancer four months earlier. She had had chemotherapy and radiation, and a visiting nurse would come by three times a week to administer medication.

Olivia's children, grandchildren, and extended family were taking good care of her. But she wanted more. She wanted to be part of the community on our street. As neighbors, we often sent cards to families on the street during times of sickness or when there was a death in the family; we also brought in meals and called to see how things were going. It hurt Olivia to feel ignored. "Didn't you see the nurse parked out front?" she asked. "How could you not know I was sick?"

Her grandson was more specific: "All of you don't care, because you're white."

Ouch—that hurt, because it wasn't true. Even so, it was important for me to realize that Olivia and her family *perceived* the neglect as racially influenced. They saw a barrier, a wall that had existed between people of different skin colors and cultures for many generations. It was easy for them to see that a wall still stood between "us" and "them."

I had not known about Olivia's illness, but God had opened a door through her phone call. It was an opportunity not only to show her love and care in a time of distressing physical illness but also to break down one of the most hard-to-demolish barriers that exists in North American society.

I brought soup over. I prayed for healing with Olivia and her family. I let others on our street know about her condition so that they could care for their neighbor as well. I also prayed that God would tear down that wall in people's minds—on both sides of the barrier.

Are there people on your street or at work who may be seeing an invisible barrier between you and them, just because of a difference in skin color or background or culture or economic status? Let Jesus' love be the instrument to break down that "dividing wall of hostility."

Don't wait to hear someone's words of hurt or anger before you think of ways to show that, for you at least, the barrier between you has come down. Take that first step of friendliness and caring. Jesus will show you how easily those walls can disappear; he has already "destroyed the barrier" through his finished work on the cross. Follow him.

—EB

Reflect/Act

- Ask God to bring to mind someone you know who may be separated from others by real or perceived walls of prejudice. What can you do to help show that person that for you the walls have already come down?
- Are there walls that still remain in your heart, walls that close out other people because of their differences? If so, ask God to show you these barriers this week.

Prayer-Starters for Praying Ephesians 2:11-18

Praise Jesus for the immense power of his blood shed on the cross, which is able to draw those who are without hope and without God in the world.

Confess any tendency you may have to forget that you also were once alienated from God, and that you may be looking down on others who are not yet believers.

Thank Jesus for becoming the peace between you and others and for breaking down the dividing walls of hostility.

Ask God to use you in breaking down any walls that may exist in your relationships with others.

Pray a BLESSing on those who live or work near you:

Body. Pray that God will use the perceived differences, disabilities, or weaknesses of others to reveal his overwhelming love and power (2 Corinthians 12:9-10), and that these qualities will not become barriers that separate your neighbors from others.

Labor. Pray that your neighbors and co-workers will not suffer from discrimination because of any perceived differences in appearance, culture, or social status.

Emotional. Ask God to help your neighbors recognize circumstances in which perceived barriers between them and others may not be there at all.

Social. Ask God to help your neighbors overcome barriers of hostility in their own family relationships or in troubled relationships at work, through coming to know Christ and growing closer to him every day.

Spiritual. Ask God to bring your neighbors to faith in Christ so that they can be "clothed . . . with Christ" and become part of the family in which "there is neither Jew nor Greek, slave nor free, male nor female, for you are all one in Christ Jesus" (Galatians 3:27-28).

DAY 5

Those Simple Little Things

"I was hungry and you gave me something to eat, I was thirsty and you gave me something to drink, I was a stranger and you invited me in . . . ."
Matthew 25:35

She was a person who had responded to the challenge to pray for her neighbors. And she was doing it faithfully, praying for three of them each day. But nothing seemed to happen.

One day, as she was driving by a craft store, she felt an urge to stop. This was very unusual, for she was not handy and never did crafts. She had no idea why she stopped and spent ten or fifteen minutes looking around. Although it was September, she found some small Christmas wreaths and impulsively bought three of them. When she got to the car, she wondered what in the world she had done that for! But she took them home, put them in her closet, and soon forgot about them.

She continued to pray faithfully for the neighbors on her list throughout the fall. During this time, though, she didn't attempt to contact them, so she didn't know what was happening in their lives. As December came, she thought it was time to contact these neighbors, and she wondered how she could let them know she had been praying for them. Then suddenly it dawned on her—God had already prepared the way! She would call on each home and give the neighbors one of those Christmas wreaths she had bought in September, and then she would tell these people she had been praying for them.

She took her six-year-old son along as she made the calls, and the first two visits were easy. These neighbors were Christians and were grateful that she had been praying for them. But she dreaded making the last call, for the third neighbor she had been praying for had always been crabby. She had always lived like a hermit, not wanting contact with anyone.

Hesitantly the mom and her son rang the woman's doorbell. They were shocked when a gaunt, ghostlike form answered the door. The woman obviously had been at death's door with some illness, and her visitors were so shocked that they could hardly greet her. "I've come," the young mother stammered, "to wish you a Merry Christmas and to give you this Christmas wreath." She quickly handed the wreath to the neighbor and turned to leave.

But just then her little son interrupted. "Mom," he said, "aren't you going to tell her you've been praying for her?"

Then it was the sickly neighbor's turn to be startled. "What did you say, little boy?" she asked. "Did you say your Mom's been praying for me?"

The boy's mother affirmed that she had indeed been praying daily for her.

Then the sick neighbor said something amazing: "Do you know that I was so sick in the past few months that I nearly died? I knew that God was sparing my life because someone must have been praying for me. And I don't have any friends, so I couldn't imagine who that might be. I've been asking God for many days to bring that person to me, and now he has answered my prayer! Would you please come in and tell me why you have been praying for me?"

What a marvelous opportunity to care and share! The praying neighbor gently shared the good news of Jesus and became close friends with the woman.

Remember, the *tiny* things you do are not small in God's eyes or in the eyes of someone who is desperate for friendship. Be sensitive. Be caring. Show Jesus' love to your neighbors.

—JDV

Reflect/Act

- Has anyone ever done a simple little thing for you that meant a whole lot? How did that make you feel?
- Think of two simple things you could do for the neighbors you are praying for. Ask God to help you find the time and the opportunity to do those things.

Prayer-Starters for Praying Matthew 25:35

Praise God that he counts things done to others as done to him.

Commit yourself to meeting the real and felt needs of people around you in the name of Christ.

Thank God for people who have done things to meet your needs—prayed for you, served you, counseled you, visited you, and so on.

Ask God to help you think of ways to do things for others, and to remember to pray for those persons each day.

Pray a BLESSing on those who live or work near you:

Body. Pray for good health, energy, food, clothing, adequate exercise, and all the basic necessities of life for your neighbors.

Labor. Pray that your neighbors may do whatever God has given them to do, and that they may make a strong contribution to God's kingdom.

Emotional. Pray that your neighbors may discover the joy of doing things, even simple little things, for others.

Social. Pray that your neighbors may be relationally sensitive and careful not to abuse, in any way, the people around them.

Spiritual. Pray that on judgment day, when God will say to his children, "Come . . . take your inheritance" (Matthew 25:34), your neighbors may be among them.

A SUGGESTION FOR MINISTRY ACTIVITY

Showing Christ's Love

Now that you have been thinking about care ministries for a few weeks, give some thought to specific ways in which you can show Christ's love to your neighbors. Here's a list of the kinds of things *Light-House* members do for their neighbors:

- offer to care for a pet for vacationing neighbors
- loan a helpful gardening tool
- help a neighbor with yard work
- provide childcare for a neighbor
- pick up trash lying around the neighborhood
- make yourself available for emergency transportation
- shovel snow off your neighbor's driveway
- give toys that your children have outgrown to a needy family
- offer to go for a short walk with an elderly neighbor
- help a neighbor with minor repair work
- give away some garden produce
- offer clothing that your children have outgrown to other neighbors with children
- love your neighbor as you love yourself

Turning Words into Actions

DAY 1

Prayer, Care, Action

Jesus looked up and said, "Father, I thank you that you have heard me. I knew that you always hear me, but I said this for the benefit of the people standing here, that they may believe that you sent me."

When he had said this, Jesus called in a loud voice, "Lazarus, come out!"

John 11:41-43

In the middle of each *Light-House* seminar I lead, I ask participants to write down the names of five neighbors, work associates, or acquaintances and to spend five minutes, right there, praying for them. After the prayer time I ask, "What did you experience in your prayer time?"

The responses people give, as they tell the whole group about these brief experiences, always amaze me. They tell of feeling "compassion," "love welling up," "burden," "empathy," and "gratitude" for the neighbors they have prayed for. They say they "are drawn to them," "want to get to know them," and "are motivated to do something." They see themselves as "divinely positioned to reach out" to their neighbors and "ready to take time with them." They become aware of their neighbors' "lostness" and "that they matter to God." All of this takes place in just five minutes of praying.

What becomes clear to me through responses to this exercise is that praying leads to caring—or, to say it the other way around, *caring flows out of praying.* As water in an artesian well flows naturally to the surface, so love flows naturally from the heart of a "pray-er"—and motivation to action soon follows.

Jesus' raising of Lazarus begins with prayer. He has been praying about Lazarus even before he arrives in Bethany, for he says, "Father, I thank you that you *have* heard me." And as he arrives, Jesus' loving, caring concern for his friends is evident. He is "deeply moved in spirit" (v. 33), and moments later he is in tears (v. 35). Soon, though, he is taking action as he stands by Lazarus's grave and calls for him to "come out."

In Jesus we see a prayer-care-action pattern that is meant to be followed as we reach out to our neighbors and friends. We begin by praying. Then caring follows as love for them wells up in our hearts. And then we are motivated to act in some way on our neighbors' behalf.

Caring begins in prayer. As you pray for your neighbors, be alert to what happens in your own heart. Do you feel compassion? Do you feel a burden for their spiritual well-being? Do you feel drawn to them? Are you ready to spend some time with them? Do you sense how much they matter to God?

Then action flows from caring. Are you motivated to do something for them? Follow the promptings of your heart as the Spirit of God leads you to reach out in caring ways to the people around you. Act on their behalf in ways that show the love of Christ. This is the biblical pattern.

—AVG

Reflect/Act

- Identify and write down the feelings that surface as you pray for your friends and neighbors.
- Act on the promptings you believe to be in line with God's will.

Prayer-Starters for Praying John 11:41-43

Thank God for his willingness to hear our prayers for others and to use us in providing for their needs.

Confess any uncaring attitudes toward neighbors that you may have had.

Ask God to fill your heart with love for those around you and to motivate you to act with love on their behalf.

Commit yourself to act on behalf of others as the Holy Spirit prompts you.

Pray a BLESSing on those who live or work near you:

Body. Pray for these neighbors' physical health and strength.

Labor. Pray that their work at home, at school, or on the job may be stimulating and satisfying.

Emotional. Pray that the peace of God that surpasses understanding will guard your neighbors' hearts and minds in Christ Jesus (Philippians 4:7).

Social. Pray for many positive, loving, supportive relationships in your neighbors' lives.

Spiritual. Pray that your neighbors may come to know Jesus Christ as Lord and Savior or that their faith in Christ may be strengthened.

DAY 2

A New Command

"A new command I give you: Love one another. As I have loved you, so you must love one another. By this all men will know that you are my disciples, if you love one another."

John 13:34-35

It was said of the apostle John that, in the last days of his life, when he was too old to speak publicly for any length of time, he would simply address congregations by saying, "Little children, love one another." His listeners, weary of his constant repetition of this phrase, asked why he always said this. "Because," he replied, "it is the Lord's command, and if it only be fulfilled, it is enough."

It was, in fact, the Lord's farewell command to his followers. Jesus said, "A new command I give you: Love one another. As I have loved you, so you must love one another" (John 13:34). These words establish a simple, yet profound, standard for the Christian's life and witness.

The word Jesus used for "love" was *agape.* It means a love that gives, a love that desires to bless, to enrich, and to lift up a person. It's a kind of love that places supreme value on the other person and acts accordingly. It's more than an emotion. This love is an act of the will, a choice. It's not the kind of love the world is used to thinking about.

In commanding us to love as he loved, Jesus is calling our attention not to the lessons he taught us but to the example of his life. Jesus' love was self-giving love. He didn't come seeking glory, position, or power for himself. He came to give himself and his life for the benefit of others. He came to seek and save the lost, and he did it by laying down his life. (See Luke 19:10; John 10:11.)

Jesus had time to love. He had time for little children, for hurting people, and for the weak and helpless. Though he was carrying out the Father's will in the world's most important mission, he was never too busy for people and their needs. Jesus' love was constant and unwavering. That's the standard he set. That's the pattern he asks us to follow.

The love of Christ, which sets the standard, also provides the motive. It's because Jesus has loved us and saved us that we are able and willing to give of our lives in love for others. Jesus' love is a transforming love. Through Jesus' love and the work of his Holy Spirit, our old love of self is transformed to love of others for Jesus' sake.

Today a love-starved, hurting world is watching to see if we, who profess to know the love of Christ, will love as Christ has loved. And Christ, in speaking these words, gave the world the right to conclude that we are his disciples if they see his love in us and experience it through us.

—AVG

Reflect/Act

- Are there ways in which you are loving others as Christ has loved you? Try to identify some specific examples.
- Think of the people around you, including your neighbors. Do you place supreme value on them and act accordingly?
- Consider possible ways in which you could bless, enrich, and lift up the lives of persons you are praying for.

Prayer-Starters for Praying Matthew 20:25-28

Praise God for sending us a loving Savior in the person of his Son.

Thank the Lord Jesus that he counts you as supremely valuable and loves you accordingly.

Confess any unloving behavior, any times when you may have been overly concerned for yourself and did not value the people around you.

Ask the Lord to fill you to overflowing with his love and to enable you to love others with his kind of love.

Pray a BLESSing on the neighbors who live or work near you:

Body. Pray for neighbors and co-workers who are fighting illnesses and pain. Ask that they may experience refreshment and relief.

Labor. Pray for neighbors who are dealing with a loss of work, income, or sense of purpose in their work. Ask God to go before them and lead them as they seek adequate, meaningful employment.

Emotional. Pray for neighbors who are emotionally distressed, grieving, sad, or depressed. Seek for them the peace of God that passes understanding (Philippians 4:7).

Social. Jesus said, "Let the little children come to me, and do not hinder them" (Matthew 19:14). Pray that the children in your neighborhood will have opportunities to learn about Jesus. Ask also that your neighbors may experience the love of Jesus in relationships with his followers.

Spiritual. Pray that God will build up the households around you into households of faith and freedom, where the love of Jesus flows freely from one person to another.

DAY 3

It's Party Time!

While Jesus was having dinner at Matthew's house, many tax collectors and "sinners" came and ate with him and his disciples.

Matthew 9:10

Jesus loved a good party!

This simple fact is often lost in our portraits of the Savior. Of course, he was serious about the problems of sin and suffering. But he also enjoyed having a good time. God, after all, was the One who created fun and enjoyment of life.

One of those occasions was the gathering that Matthew put together for him, after Jesus had called Matthew to be one of his followers. Matthew's friends, of course, were not the most respected people in society; they were tax collectors and other known sinners of that day. But they were still Matthew's friends, so he threw a party and invited them to celebrate the fact that he was going to be a disciple of Jesus. And, of course, Jesus came, since the party probably was in his honor.

The Pharisees, however, the religious fanatics of that day, looked on with their sour faces and were offended that Jesus not only went to parties but also spent time with folks who had questionable reputations. It's good for us to remember this. For, as Christians, we can get so "heavy" at times that we forget this "lighter side" of the nature of our Savior. Caring for people not only means meeting their "need to be needed"; it also means bringing light, fun, and laughter into their lives.

In one of his books Tony Campolo tells an interesting story about something that happened to him in Hawaii. He could not sleep one night, so at three in the morning he went out to a local restaurant to get something to eat. Shortly after he sat down, a group of six or eight women came in and ordered dinner. He asked the proprietor who they were, and he was told they were prostitutes who had just finished their work for the night. They came in at about the same time every night. Tony also overheard one of them say, rather sadly, that tomorrow would be her birthday but that no one really cared.

Tony got an idea. He asked the proprietor if he would be interested in throwing a birthday party the next day—a surprise party. The proprietor grinned. The idea sounded great to him. Tony bought a great big, special birthday cake, and the restaurant owner fixed a special meal and decorated the place. When the women came in the next morning, Tony and the owner shouted, "Surprise!"

The women, of course, where utterly shocked. Tony and the proprietor presented the "birthday girl" with the cake and candles and then asked her to cut it. But she refused. Instead, with tears rolling down her cheeks, she said, "Do you mind if I just take it home with me? Whole? This is the first birthday cake I ever got in my life, and I want to just look at it for a few days!"

People are desperate for lightness and fun. As Christians, we are called to be guides to true happiness. In your caring for others, be lighthearted today. Bring some laughter and joy. Throw a party. And be sure to invite Jesus. He loves a good party!

—JDV

Reflect/Act

- Think of people you know who seem to be desperate for fun. What kinds of things could you do to bring some laughter and joy into their lives?

Prayer-Starters for Praying Matthew 9:10

Praise God that he has a "lighter side" and is eager to provide joy and happiness to his children.

Ask God for the ability and the opportunity to bring joy and laughter into someone else's life.

Thank God for the joy and peace he has brought into your life through Jesus Christ, and spread some of your joy around today.

Pray a BLESSing on people you know:

Body. The Bible says that "a cheerful heart is good medicine" (Proverbs 17:22). Pray that God will give this medicine to some unhappy people you know.

Labor. Pray that your neighbors may be grateful for the employer and the work they have. If they are without work, ask God to grant them the joy of meaningful employment.

Emotional. Pray that your neighbors and friends may find joy in life and in the Lord.

Social. Pray that good relationships may bring joy to the people around you.

Spiritual. Pray that your neighbors may come to the Lord and find true happiness in him.

DAY 4

Listening to God

"When he, the Spirit of truth, comes, he will guide you into all truth. He will not speak on his own; he will speak only what he hears, and he will tell you what is yet to come."

John 16:13

How can you tell when God speaks to you? Do you ever wonder about people who confidently say, "Well, God told me to do this or that . . ."? How do they know?

Without a doubt there is spiritual abuse among people who claim to hear God talking to them. But the Bible tells us clearly that Jesus' gift to us as believers is the Spirit of God within us. And since the Spirit lives both in the mind of the Father and in our own minds, he can communicate and guide us with the very thoughts of God. The only problem is to find how we can know that the ideas we get are not from our own sinful nature or from the devil but from God. Here's a true story that shows a way in which some missionaries have heard God speaking to their hearts.

Mary Ghee was a missionary to India in the 1950s. She worked as a teacher for almost two years in a village but had little success bringing anyone to Christ. Then Dr. Scudder, a missionary doctor, visited the village for a week, and during his visit many amazing things happened. This perplexed Mary's Indian neighbors. "Why," they asked her, "does your God work miracles when Dr. Scudder comes? You have been among us for nearly two years, and yet very few things have happened." How would you respond?

Mary asked Dr. Scudder what he did. The doctor said that whenever he presented a problem to the Lord, he would ask God to "shut off" his sinful desires and the voice of the devil. Then he would wait, and he would write down the first thing that came to his mind. And if it was in line with Scripture, he concluded that God was speaking to him, so he went out and did it.

Mary was having a problem with her neighbor, so early one morning she tried this approach as she prayed: "God, I am going to listen and write down the first thing you tell me to do to solve this problem with my neighbor." She waited, with pencil and paper ready. Suddenly a thought came: "Take her an egg." Mary thought about this. Her neighbor was a widow with ten children. How embarrassing it would be to take just one egg! So she wrinkled up the paper, threw it away, and went to do her teaching for the morning.

That noon, when she came home, Mary found that a chicken had found its way into her house and was resting on one of her chairs. Then, when she shooed it away, she saw that it had laid an egg on the chair. "All right, Lord," Mary said, "I get the message." She took the egg to her neighbor's house and gave it to one of the woman's little boys, who was playing outside.

The next morning the neighbor came to Mary's house and asked, "Why did you give me that egg yesterday, Mary?" With embarrassment, Mary told her how she had been trying to listen to the Lord to solve the problem they were having. "Mary!" said her neighbor excitedly. "You know how poor I am. Yesterday I had given all my food to my children, and in the morning I prayed, 'God, if you will only give me one egg, I can make it through the day.' God used you to bring me that egg!" From that point on, Mary and her neighbor stopped their fighting. God worked his miracle of reconciliation.

Don't discount an answer you may be receiving from God because it seems not to make any sense. God answers us in many ways, and we can always search his Word, the Bible, for guidance when we think we hear God speaking to us. Just be aware that God may be speaking to you in surprising ways. Remember Joshua and the battle of Jericho (Joshua 5:13-6:27). Remember Gideon (Judges 6-7). Remember Peter and Cornelius (Acts 10).

As long as the answer you hear seems to help or show love to someone, do what God gently inclines your mind to do in caring for others. Some very imaginative things may happen. But don't be afraid to follow your inclinations, for God may have some marvelous surprises in store for you.

—JDV

Reflect/Act

- Reflect briefly on the fact that God knows the answers to all your questions. Ask God for guidance on a specific concern you have and then give him time to impress you with his thoughts as you wait.

Prayer-Starters for Praying John 16:13

Praise God, who guides us into all truth.

Confess to the Lord any tendency you may have to move ahead on your own without seeking his guidance.

Commit all your ways to the Lord.

Ask to be filled with the knowledge of God's will.

Pray a blessing on your neighbors, using Proverbs 3:5-7:

Pray that your neighbors will learn to "trust in the Lord with all [their] heart and not lean on [their] own understanding."

Pray that your neighbors will "acknowledge the Lord" in all their ways.

Reaching Out a Hand

*This is how we know what love is: Jesus Christ laid down his life for us.
And we ought to lay down our lives for our brothers. If anyone has
material possessions and sees his brother in need but has no pity on
him, how can the love of God be in him?*

1 John 3:16-17

"The beautiful IDS Building towers over the skyline of Minneapolis. Its fifty-seven stories of blue-black glass make an impressive sight.

"One day, a depressed executive opened the doors of his fifteenth-story office, walked out on the ledge, and threatened to leap to his death.

"A Christian friend, who happened to be present, pleaded with the man not to take his own life.

"Teetering on the edge, the executive said, 'If you really mean it—will you come over and take my hand?'

"The Christian man, realizing his friend could drag both of them over the edge—hesitated.

"When the businessman saw the hesitation, he said, 'You're just like the rest. You talk, but you don't really care.' Then he turned and leaped to his death."

—adapted from *Heart for the Harvest* by Lowell Lundstrom

What Jesus did for us was more than talk. It was more than showing us how to live as God wants us to. He really cared! He cared so much for us that he "laid down his life for us." Finding us in a hopeless state of despair and spiritual death, Jesus reached out his hand and drew us back to safety. "This is how we know what love is."

Jesus now asks us to be willing to do for others as he did for us. "We ought to lay down our lives for our brothers," says John. That's a mighty big challenge!

Does this mean we have to die to prove our love for others? No, although some of us may be called to die to show our love *for Jesus.* John is talking here about being willing, for Jesus' sake, to do whatever is necessary to meet the needs of those around us, even to the point of death. He is challenging us to *really* care! When we're that willing and that ready to care, we will truly reflect the love of Christ.

Caring that goes beyond talk to reaching out a hand is risky business. We risk being pulled off the "comfort ledge" of our lives into something that may be

136

costly. It may cost us time. It may cost us energy. It may require giving up some of our treasured freedom. It may also cost us money or material goods.

Our willingness to part with something we value for Jesus' sake and to give it to people who are in need is a sign that the love of God is in us. This is how love shows itself. The evidence is on display in whatever we do.

We live in a very hurting world. It's a world full of opportunities to care, and in our caring we have all kinds of opportunities to showcase Jesus' love to the people around us.

Is there a showcase of God's love in your neighborhood?

—AVG

Reflect/Act

- Think of a time when someone reached out a hand to you. What does it tell you about that person? About God?
- Think of needs and hurts in the lives of the people around you that may give you an opportunity to reach out to them.

Prayer-Starters for 1 John 3:16-17

Praise Jesus for the love that caused him to lay down his life for you. *Thank* him for doing that.

Confess any failings you may have had in reaching out a loving hand to another person.

Ask God to help you see the needs of people around you and to give you a heart willing to pay the cost of reaching out.

Pray a BLESSing on neighbors who live or work near you:

Body. Offer yourself to be used by God to help meet the needs of the people around you.

Labor. Pray that neighbors will work diligently and handle their financial resources wisely so that they may give of their resources to reach out to others.

Emotional. Pray that hurting people may have the grace to admit their need for help and allow others to help them.

Social. Pray that parents may be willing to give of themselves for their children, and that friends and neighbors may be willing to give of themselves for each other.

Spiritual. Pray that your neighbors will come to know God's love and be willing to take hold of his loving hand outstretched to them.

How Do I Share with My Neighbors?

by David J. Deters

Contents

Who's Doing the Work?

DAY 1

I'm Terrified

Moses said to the Lord, "O Lord, I have never been eloquent, neither in the past nor since you have spoken to your servant. I am slow of speech and tongue."

The Lord said to him, "Who gave man his mouth? Who makes him deaf or mute? Who gives him sight or makes him blind? Is it not I, the Lord? Now go; I will help you speak and will teach you what to say."

Exodus 4:10-12

I'll admit it, first thing: *Sharing with my neighbors terrifies me.* That's right. I pray for my neighbors; I care about them. But to share my faith with them just downright terrifies me.

I'm not sure I even understand why. In the past I've talked with my neighbors about politics. They know what I do professionally. We've shared lawn and carpentry tools. I've brought them meals when they've been sick; they've returned the favor. I've visited them when they've been hospitalized. Some of us even exchange Christmas and birthday cards and gifts. We know a lot about each other's families and friends. I've even been asked to officiate at memorial services for family pets. But, for some reason, talking with my neighbors about my relationship with Christ is something that makes my heart go into overdrive.

There are a lot of reasons for this, I suppose. God is very important to me, and I want my neighbors to know about him—but what if I give them the wrong information? And what approach do I take? I certainly don't want to come off as "preachy." And what if I completely blow it? I may only get one chance. If I don't get it right, there goes their whole eternity!

There are lots of reasons why we don't share our faith with our neighbors. But one of the main reasons is that we are just too afraid. And our fear may come from a notion that sharing our faith puts us in a position of too much responsibility—more than we can handle. We don't feel capable of helping God bring the miracle of new life. Some of us really believe that it's up to us alone to bring our neighbors into a personal relationship with God.

As you begin to move from praying, to caring, to actually sharing the good news of Jesus with your neighbor, always remember who takes the ultimate responsibility for your neighbor's response. It's not you. The One responsible for the miracle of new life is God alone.

Through his Holy Spirit, God is already at work in the heart of your neighbor. And God is already at work in you. Your job is simply to be available as the voice box for the words the Holy Spirit will give you to speak. You aren't the one who will change your neighbor's heart. You aren't the one who will cause him or her to cross the line from mis-belief to belief in Jesus. That's God's job. He simply invites you to work alongside him.

Reflect/Act

- How responsive are you to the leading of God the Holy Spirit in your life?
- What are some of the specific ways in which God has done an unexpected, miraculous thing in your life?

Prayer-Starters for Praying Exodus 4:10-12

Praise God by letting him know how thankful you are that he is in control. God is the One who gave you your mouth, your mind, your eyes, your ears. God is the One who has a perfect plan for your life and for the lives of your neighbors.

Ask God to calm your fears and settle your anxieties about sharing with your neighbor. Ask him to give you the words to speak.

Thank God that he loves you and your neighbor more than any of us could ever imagine. The Lord's desire is to share eternity with us. He has done everything necessary to make that possible.

Pray a BLESSing on the neighbors who live or work near you:

Remember that the word *BLESS* here serves as a reminder of five vital areas in our lives.

Body. Pray that you may be a blessing to your neighbors by helping with any physical needs they might have.

Labor. Ask God to help your neighbors serve him through their work today, doing all they can to the glory of God (Colossians 3:23).

Emotional. Ask that your neighbors may not be burdened by any worries or anxieties but have "the peace of God, which transcends all understanding" (Philippians 4:6-7).

Social. Ask God to provide opportunities for your neighbors to meet with and talk with believers like you about Jesus and his good news.

Spiritual. Pray that your unsaved neighbors will come to know Christ through faithful witnesses of his love. Ask that God will use you to share the good news of Jesus with your neighbors.

DAY 2

"On Beyond Zebra"

Jesus said . . . "How hard it is to enter the kingdom of God! It is easier for a camel to go through the eye of a needle than for a rich man to enter the kingdom of God."

The disciples . . . said to each other, "Who then can be saved?"

Jesus . . . said, "With man this is impossible, but not with God; all things are possible with God."

Mark 10:24-27

I'm a little embarrassed to say this, but one of my favorite authors is Theodor Geisel, also known as Dr. Seuss. That's right—one of my favorite authors is a children's writer. Dr. Seuss was a master of helping us to see and understand big and amazing things in simple, childlike ways.

One of my favorite stories by Dr. Seuss is "On Beyond Zebra." In this story a boy is showing another boy how to spell: "The A is for Ape. And the B is for Bear. The C is for Camel. The H is for Hare. The M is for Mouse. And the R is for Rat. I know all the twenty-six letters like that." But that wasn't enough for this boy. He found it necessary to go "on beyond Z," or, "on beyond Zebra." "In the places I go," he said, "there are things that I see that I never could spell if I stopped with the Z."

And do you know what? That's absolutely true in our relationship with God. Our little alphabet is completely inadequate when it comes to describing God, especially when it comes to describing what God has done for your and my salvation—and our neighbors'. Jesus says, simply and clearly, "All things are possible with God." This means God can do things in your neighbor's life that are beyond description. In fact, God can do things that are "on beyond" our imagination—including things he can do for your neighbors through people like you and me (Ephesians 3:20).

"But you don't know my neighbor!" you might be saying. That's true. I don't know your neighbor. I don't know the pain he or she has had. I don't know how thick your neighbor's skin is against the work of the Holy Spirit. I don't know how skilled your neighbor is in tying your thoughts into knots when you try to share your faith with him. I don't know your neighbor and the unique challenge she is for you.

But I do know something about God. God can do the impossible. He saved you and me. He also has the desire to save your neighbor. These are miracles we can't begin to describe! And God is the One who does them!

Sometimes we need to be reminded of that. God doesn't expect us to do miracles. He simply wants us to pray for our neighbors, show them we care, and share his message of good news in Jesus. God wants us to live as examples of Jesus' love for our neighbors.

As we pray for our neighbors, God's Spirit works at preparing their hearts to receive him. As we pray, God's Spirit also works in us to give us the compassion and care for our neighbors that God himself has. And in the meantime God prepares opportunities for us to spend time with and talk with our neighbors. All we have to do is be faithful, listening, looking for needs to be filled, and sharing about how much God means to us. And in God's strength we can do that (Philippians 4:13)!

Let God work through you in surprising ways. God's love for you and your neighbor in his wonder-filled life for you goes "on beyond Zebra"!

Reflect/Act

- How has God been "on beyond Zebra" in your life? Make a list of four or five ways in which God has been this way in our world and in your life.
- Commit to praying earnestly for your neighbors this week, and if God presents you with opportunities, share your love for the Lord with your neighbors.

Prayer-Starters for Praying Mark 10:24-27

Praise God that his grace reaches all the way into your life, into your neighborhood, and into the lives of each person you will meet today.

Ask God to fill you with a love that is "on beyond Zebra." *Ask* God to give you his love for your neighbor.

Thank God that he is able to do the impossible. *Thank* God, too, for his desire to do the impossible in your life and in your neighbors' lives.

Pray a BLESSing on your neighbors who live or work near you:

Body. Be courageous. Be daring. Ask God to bring bodily healing into the lives of your neighbors.

Labor. Ask that something "on beyond Zebra" might happen in your neighbors' work on the job, at school, or at home.

Emotional. Pray that your next-door neighbors, co-workers, or classmates may sense a joy that causes them to wonder who its source is.

Social. Ask God to bring quality friendships into your neighbors' lives. Pray that your relationships with them may grow.

Spiritual. Pray that God's grace may overwhelm all the people in your life. "God so loved the world that he gave his one and only Son" for everyone who believes (John 3:16)! That's "on beyond Zebra"!

DAY 3

"God So Loved the World"

"God so loved the world that he gave his one and only Son, that whoever believes in him shall not perish but have eternal life. For God did not send his Son into the world to condemn the world, but to save the world through him."

John 3:16-17

"God so loved _____ that he gave his one and only Son . . . ."

Go ahead. Put your name in the blank space. It's a perfectly legitimate thing to do. In fact, it's a critically important thing to do.

God so loves this world that "he gave his one and only Son." God's love is focused on this world he made, on the nations and peoples of this world, and on each and every person in it. God loves you. In fact, as someone has said, "God loves each one of us as if we were the only one in all the world to love."

So put your name in the blank space and say the words of John 3:16 again. In fact, why not actually write out the verse with your name in it? If that doesn't move your heart, if that doesn't send a tremor through the foundation of your life, if that doesn't send lightning bolts into every corner of your life, I don't know what will. God loved you so much that he was willing to sacrifice himself! And he looks at you with fondness and steadfast love. God cares about you in ways you can't even imagine! He loves you more than you love yourself. God has your name printed on the palm of his hand. He knows how many hairs crown your head. He notices every tear you shed, as if he were collecting them in a bottle. God loves you!!

Now, put the name of your neighbor in the blank space of our Scripture verse. In fact, why not actually write out the verse with your neighbor's name in it? God has such a concern for your neighbor's spiritual future that he gave away his one and only Son. If that's how much God cares, then you and I ought to care too. If God is willing to make that much of a sacrifice for your neighbor, then you and I ought to be willing to step out of our comfort zones and share the good news with him or her. If that's how much God cares, then you and I ought to be willing to share that information with others.

Reflect /Act

- Knowing that you are loved is a feeling that can hardly be described. What's it like for you? How does it affect you? Think about it. God loves you. Unconditionally. Eternally. Immeasurably.
- God loves your neighbor in the same way. If you don't know the names of your neighbors, make an effort to learn them. Then write out John 3:16 with their names in the blank space. Pray that God will work in their lives and provide you with opportunities to share his love with them.

Prayer-Starters for Praying John 3:16

Praise God for his extraordinary ability to love.

Ask God to work in your life in such a way that you will be able to reflect his love for your neighbor. Ask him to love through you.

Thank God for loving you in the way he does. Thank him that nothing can separate you from his love.

Pray a BLESSing on your neighbors who live or work near you:

Body. Ask God, in his love for everything in this created world, to bless your next-door neighbors, co-workers, classmates, or other acquaintances with physical health and strength.

Labor. Pray that these neighbors may use their skills to the best of their ability and think about who gave them their skills.

Emotional. Pray that God's love may so fill your neighbors that they are free of worry and anxiety, knowing they are loved as if they were the only ones in the world for God to love.

Social. Ask God to help your neighbors love one another and all the people they come into contact with.

Spiritual. Pray that your neighbors may come to know God's love so personally and deeply that they (re)dedicate their lives to him, trusting fully in Jesus as their Savior and Lord.

More Than You Could Ask

Now to him who is able to do immeasurably more than all we ask or imagine, according to his power that is at work within us, to him be glory in the church and in Christ Jesus throughout all generations, for ever and ever! Amen.

Ephesians 3:20-21

This verse has been one of my favorites for years. It describes, layer by layer, what God is willing and able to do for us.

The apostle Paul is asking us to give glory to God for all he is willing to do for us in Christ.

Look at what God is willing to do. Paul says that God is willing to use all of his power simply to do *what we ask*. If God is willing to do that—wow!—that's amazing! And yet it's true!

But that's not all Paul is saying. God is willing to do more than that. Paul says that God is willing to use all of his power to do what we ask *or even imagine*. God is willing to fulfill even our dreams. That's fantastic!

But that's not all Paul is saying. God is willing to do more than that. Paul says that God is willing to use all of his power to do "*more* than all we ask or imagine." God is willing to go beyond what we even think or dream. That's stupendous!

But even that's not all. God is willing to do even more. Paul says that God is willing to use all of his power to do *immeasurably* more than we ask and *immeasurably* more than we can imagine. God is willing to go immeasurably beyond what I ask or dream. Now that's utterly mind-boggling!

Just think about it. God is ready and willing to come alongside you and invest infinitely more energy than you can imagine to help you share his message of love with your neighbor. I don't know about you, but that makes me want to give glory to God.

Amen? Amen!

Reflect/Act

- God wants to do more than all you could ask or imagine for your neighborhood, your workplace, your school, or wherever you interact with people. Use your imagination to dream up some things you would like to see God do for your neighbors in these places, to his glory.
- God has done the immeasurable for you! Make a list of God's blessings in your life, and ask him to help you share your thoughts about his greatness with a neighbor.

Prayer-Starters for Praying Ephesians 3:20-21

Praise God for his immeasurable love for you, your neighbors, and your world. Be specific in praising God clearly for the great things he has done.

Ask God to provide your neighbors with more than you can ask or imagine. Keep a prayer journal, writing your requests for your neighbors in it regularly. As the days and weeks go by, you'll want to know how God answers your specific prayers.

Thank God for his commitment to you and to everyone else who lives on this earth. God's gift of salvation—earned for us through the life, death, and resurrection of God's "one and only Son" (John 3:16)—is more than we could ever ask or imagine.

Pray a blessing on your neighbors, using Ephesians 3:16-21:

With the apostle Paul, pray that out of God's "glorious riches" your neighbors may be strengthened "with power through his Spirit" in their inner being, so that Christ may live in their hearts through faith.

Ask that your neighbors may be "rooted and established in love" so that they "may have power . . . to grasp how wide and long and high and deep is the love of Christ."

Pray that your neighbors, knowing this love, "may be filled to the measure of all the fullness of God."

Ask God to move your neighbors to trust that he can "do immeasurably more than all we ask or imagine," and that by God's power at work in them, your neighbors may bring him glory forever.

DAY 5

Hide and Seek

"The Son of Man came to seek and to save what was lost."

Luke 19:10

This verse in Luke 19 closes the great story about Jesus and his meeting with Zacchaeus. It's a delightful story about the Savior taking time to share his love with one human being. Frederick Buechner describes the encounter this way:

> Zacchaeus stood barely five feet tall with his shoes off and was the least popular man in Jericho. He was head tax-collector for Rome in the district and had made such a killing out of it that he was the richest man in town as well as the shortest. When word got around that Jesus would soon be passing through, he shinnied up into a sycamore tree so he could see something more than just the backs of other people's heads, and that's where he was when Jesus spotted him.
>
> —*Peculiar Treasures,* pp. 179-180

The idea of the Son of Man taking the time to notice, in a life-changing way, one short, socially outcast man proves Jesus' commitment to the mission of seeking and finding the lost.

There aren't too many uses for the word *seek* in our everyday language today—except maybe in this verse (Luke 19:10) and in the children's game "Hide and Seek." That game illustrates the meaning of God's desire. He declares himself "it." And you and I—and our neighbors—have taken our hearts, minds, and bodies into hiding. (See Genesis 3:8-9.) But Jesus won't quit until the game is finished and he has sought out and found everyone who belongs to him. It's his game, his mission. And when he finds us, he saves us and invites us to come alongside to play and work with him.

When God saves us, we belong to him, and he protects us. When God saves us, he won't let anyone else touch us. When God saves us, no one will ever be able to snatch us out of his hands (John 10:29).

What kinds of things can you do in your neighborhood, your workplace, your school—wherever you are—to play and work with God as he seeks out people who are hiding from him and need to be found? Maybe there's someone you know who doesn't know Jesus. Or maybe you're not sure whether that person knows Jesus. Make an effort to get to know that person better, to find out what he or she really does believe and why.

Start with prayer, asking God to open your own heart to love this person as Jesus does. Listen as God speaks to you, leading you in what to do next. Ask God to provide an opportunity for you to meet with or call on this person.

Perhaps you could meet at a restaurant, go walking or biking together, or work on a backyard project together. Or you could simply invite this person to share some social time over a cup of coffee at your home.

With God's help, search out ways to show that you care, to show that you want to develop a relationship. This person needs to be able to trust you and get to know you so that he or she can grow to trust in God.

Reflect/Act

• To label yourself as a "sinner" is almost okay in our culture today. Few of us would claim to be sinless. But to be "lost"? As an adult? That's a different matter. What does it feel like to be lost? How do you react when someone you care about is lost? Take the time to answer these questions and apply them to your desires for your neighbors.

Prayer-Starters for Praying Luke 19:10

Thank God that he is just as willing to look for us as he was willing to look for Zacchaeus.

Talk with God about areas in which you may be hiding. *Confess* any efforts you may be making to control certain areas of your life, and ask God to help you give your entire being to him.

Ask God to keep looking for your unsaved neighbors and to help you pray for them and get to know them better.

Thank God for his persistence in looking for us, finding us, and keeping us safe in his care.

Pray a BLESSing on your hiding neighbors who need to be found:

Body. Pray that your neighbors may hear God's voice calling them and that they may grow to depend on God for every physical need.

Labor. Ask God to speak to your neighbors in some way through the work they do today.

Emotional. Ask that your neighbors may trust God and be freed from any fear they might have that they cannot be forgiven of their sins.

Social. Pray that the Lord will use people today to search out your neighbors who need to be found and introduced to his love.

Spiritual. Pray that the persons for whom you have been praying may have an amazing, life-changing experience with God soon!

A FAITH-SHARING METHOD

Evangelism means "bringing the message of good news." In this third section of *Developing a Prayer-Care-Share Lifestyle* our focus is on sharing the good news of Jesus with persons who are ready to receive it, thanks to the preparing work of the Holy Spirit.

To offer some practical help on sharing your faith, we've included several examples of faith-sharing methods in between the weekly sets of readings here. Not everyone uses the same approach to sharing the gospel ("good news"), so you will probably find that one or two of these methods suits you better than the others. If you're ready, in God's strength, to share the good news of Jesus with a neighbor, check out these methods to see which one(s) may work best for you.

Using a Small Book— *How to Talk to God*

Houses of Prayer Everywhere (HOPE) makes available a gospel-presentation booklet called *How to Talk to God.* The premise of this book is that people who are ready to take the faith step need to start talking to God.

But not just any talk will do! People need to tell God they are sorry for sins, that they accept his offer of salvation in Jesus, and that they are ready to serve him with their lives. The booklet *How to Talk to God* helps them know what to say as they begin talking to God.

Steps in Using *How to Talk to God*

1. Give the booklet to inquirers or anyone who is showing some interest in knowing what it means to have a relationship with God. Of course, you'll need to become familiar with the booklet yourself before recommending it to anyone. As you hand people the booklet,

- tell them how it helped you understand about talking to God.
- encourage them to read it and to make note of anything they may have questions about.

2. Promise to get back to them to talk about what they read and to answer any questions they might have.

- Set a time for this visit, if possible.

3. Get back to them and ask if they have read the booklet. If not, encourage them again to read it, and then set a new time to return. Once they have read it, engage them in conversation about the content:

- Did it make sense to them?
- Did they have any questions?
- Did they pray the prayer at the end of the booklet? If so . . .

4. Rejoice with them and remind them that they are now friends of God. If they have not prayed the prayer, try to learn why. Be ready to help them understand and pray the prayer.

5. Encourage those who have started praying to spend as much time as possible talking to God. That's the way the relationship will grow.

6. Urge them to share their experience and their booklet with someone else who may want to start a relationship with God.

To order *How to Talk to God*, call HOPE at 1-800-217-5200.

Develop a Relationship

Developing a Relationship

The Lord said to Cain, "Where is your brother Abel?"
"I don't know," he replied. "Am I my brother's keeper?"

Genesis 4:9-10

Yes, you are your brother and sister's keeper. The essence of being a Christian is a relationship—a personal, one-on-one relationship with God. And God calls us to "love one another"—even our enemies (John 13:34; Matthew 5:44-45). So being a Christian also involves relationships with all other human beings—for all are created in God's image (Genesis 1:26-27).

Relationships take time. They take energy; they take commitment; they involve risk. Relationships can bring incredible blessings; they can also bring excruciating pain. God has experienced all of these in his relationship with each one of us.

The same can happen to you as you take the step of sharing the gospel—the good news of Jesus—with your neighbors. I'm not going to sugarcoat this one. If you want to involve yourself in one of the greatest experiences of the Christian life—realizing that the Spirit of Christ has used you in some significant way to make an impact on one of your neighbors for the Lord for eternity—it will cost you.

All relationships involve a healthy investment. In the next several days we're going to look at how you can begin to make such an investment. But before we start, it's critical that you place yourself in the hands of the God who promises to walk alongside you. Place yourself in the hands of the One who has already made the ultimate investment in your life and in the life of your neighbor.

It's important to know that your neighbor is a person of inestimable value. Your neighbor matters to God. Your neighbor is precious to Christ, who was willing to sacrifice his own life for him or her.

If that's how valuable your neighbor is to God; if he or she matters that much to God, then you and I need to make the commitment to treat that neighbor with love and sensitivity. If God loves your neighbor that much, then the time, the energy, the joy, and even the possible pain or discomfort of developing a relationship with that neighbor is a small price for you to pay.

Think about being a channel of God's love to your neighbor. Think about being an instrument God can use to reveal himself to your neighbor. Ask God today to help you pray for, care for, and share with your neighbor, entering into relationship for Jesus' sake.

God wants to do amazing things through you. Are you ready?

Reflect/Act

• God uses a variety of ways to bring us into relationship with himself. Most often, though, he chooses to introduce himself through other human beings. Take some time to reflect on how God used people to introduce you to Christ. Who were those people?

• What can you do to make yourself a more usable instrument through which God can reveal himself?

Prayer-Starters for Praying Genesis 4:9-10

Praise God for loving you as a person of inestimable value.

Thank him for the people in your life who have considered you their brother or sister in the Lord.

Confess to God any ways in which you have ignored the physical, emotional, and spiritual needs of people whom he considers to be your brothers and sisters. Ask God to forgive you for these shortcomings.

Ask God to bring to your mind the names of anyone in your relational circle (family, neighborhood, school mates, co-workers) whom he desires to adopt into his family as your spiritual brothers and sisters. When God brings names to your mind, write them down and begin praying for them.

Ask God to help you view each of your neighbors as a person of inestimable value.

Pray a BLESSing on your neighbors everywhere today:

Body. Ask God to meet your neighbors' needs for health, strength, and safety from bodily harm.

Labor. Pray that your neighbors may do their work well as a way of building on their relationship with the Lord.

Emotional. Pray that the Lord will let your neighbors know how precious they are to him, and that they may experience his peace today.

Social. Ask God to help your neighbors develop caring relationships with the people in their lives and to avoid any competitive rivalries at home, at school, or in the workplace.

Spiritual. Pray that your neighbors may experience a growing awareness of God's presence in their lives, and that he loves them and calls them to serve him and others.

DAY 2

Aware

O Lord, you have searched me and you know me. You know when I sit and when I rise; you perceive my thoughts from afar. You discern my going out and my lying down; you are familiar with all my ways.

Psalm 139:1-3

As you begin to develop a relationship with your neighbor, there are four *A's* that will help. God calls us to be *Aware, Available, Alert,* and *Accepting.* We'll talk about each of these *A's* in the next four days.

First, God calls us to be *Aware.* Always be *aware* that God loves your neighbor more than you do. God has provided for the needs of your neighbor from the riches of his eternal glory. God has a preferred future for your neighbor, filled with hope and promise. More than anything else, God wants a personal relationship with your neighbor that is every bit as intimate as the one he shares with you. God wants to give your neighbor his salvation to new life.

So as you begin to move toward the fantastic privilege of being used to introduce your neighbor to the Lord Jesus, never, ever forget that this is God's plan, God's hope, God's dream, God's desire for your neighbor. Be aware that you will play an important part in the process but that God is the One who will be saving your neighbor.

Here's an illustration that might help. Imagine God making his way down some superhighway toward your neighbor's life. Imagine yourself "merging" onto that highway and simply following the direction God has already set.

One of the things I need to remember every day of my life, and most often in my desire to be used to bring others to Christ, is that God works around the clock. Sometimes I wonder if God created us with a need to sleep so that we would be "out of the way" once in a while, so that he would be able to get some work done without our interference. Each morning, as you and I open our eyes, we need to check in with the Lord to find out just how far he has traveled down that highway while we've been sleeping. We need to be tuned in to God's working closer and closer to the heart of our neighbor's greatest need.

Celebrate the marvelous fact that God has invited you to be part of the greatest enterprise in his world: *reconciliation*—that is, restoring the relationships of men, women, and children in your neighborhood to the God who has created them and loves them!

Praise God this day for his amazing love and salvation! Praise him for his watchful care for you and your neighbors every minute of every day! Praise God for calling you to be part of his great work of renewing relationships with your neighbors!

Reflect/Act

- God is absolutely aware of every detail of every life. Celebrate that fact today. Be *aware* that nothing is held secret from God.
- Make a list of the things God has done to open the way for you and your neighbor to renew a right relationship with him. This list will heighten your awareness of just how much God has invested himself in our eternal salvation and life.

Prayer-Starters for Praying Psalm 139:1-3

Thank God for his knowledge of you and of everything about you.

Ask God to give you the courage to evaluate and confess anything in your life that you aren't pleased to have him know about. Ask God for his forgiveness and help in putting things right in your life.

Thank God for his commitment to you and your neighbor.

Ask God to help you join him in his mission to adopt your neighbor into his family and to introduce your neighbor to the Savior.

Pray a BLESSing on your neighbors:

This is a good day to review the prayers you have been offering to God for your neighbor. Repeat your prayers from last week. Add some new ones as God increases your knowledge of your neighbor's life and needs.

Body. Ask God to bless your neighbors with health, strength, and bodily healing today.

Labor. Ask God to work miracles in your neighbors' workplaces or classrooms today, and to help them see his hand working in their lives.

Emotional. Pray that your neighbor, co-worker, or classmate may experience the joy of God's presence and know his peace.

Social. Ask God to bring quality friendships into your neighbor's life, and to reveal himself to your neighbors through you and others. Pray that your relationships with your neighbors may grow.

Spiritual. Pray that God's grace may overwhelm your neighbor or co-worker. Just think of it! God so loves the world that he gave his one and only Son to restore our relationship with him!

DAY 3

Available

The LORD came and stood there, calling . . . "Samuel! Samuel!"
Then Samuel said, "Speak, for your servant is listening."
And the LORD said to Samuel: "See, I am about to do something in
Israel that will make the ears of everyone who hears of it tingle."

1 Samuel 3:10-11

When I was in junior high, my parents brought up a very important topic at the dinner table one evening. Together with me and my younger brother and sister, they wanted to make a commitment that we all silently pray a specific prayer each morning before leaving the house to go to school or work. Each of us would sincerely make ourselves *Available* to God to be used by him in the life of someone else that day. And then in the evening, at dinner, we would take turns describing the ways we had experienced God answering our prayers during the day.

Do you know what I remember from that experience? The days that began with the prayer of making ourselves available to God almost always resulted in a clear, specific answer at some point during the day. When we prayed, "God, I'm available to be used by you in the life of someone else today," God used us.

He often used us in very simple ways. Sometimes we were able to give a word of encouragement to someone who was frustrated or terribly discouraged. Sometimes we were asked very specifically for help. And then there were times when friends, classmates, and the people my parents worked with would ask specific questions about the foundation of our lives and the Christ we were trying to follow and serve.

Another thing I remember about that experience was that *the opposite was also true.* On those days when we didn't pause to make ourselves available, we most often had nothing to talk about at dinnertime.

It was a great lesson. I will always be thankful to my parents for helping me learn to pray to make myself *available* to God each day.

God doesn't force us into service. He invites us. And when we make ourselves available to him, watch out! He will take us up on our offer.

Will you pray that *availability* prayer with me today? All you have to do is pray it sincerely: "Lord, use me in any way you choose in the life of someone today. Make me available."

If you pray that prayer today, you'll have a story to tell tonight.

Reflect/Act

- Are you available? If God opened up an opportunity for you to share your faith with a neighbor or co-worker, would you know it?
- Volunteer to God for service in your neighborhood. God doesn't force people, but he does accept volunteers.

Prayer-Starters for Praying 1 Samuel 3:10-11

Ask God to speak to you. Tell him you are listening.

Ask the Holy Spirit to help you schedule the day with enough open space that if he wants to do something with and through you, you've got the time.

Thank God for the extraordinary honor he gives us to work alongside him in his kingdom. God could do all the work by himself, but in his grace he has invited us to be his co-workers. What a gift! What an honor!

Pray that you can be a blessing to others today:

In your prayers for your neighbors, co-workers, classmates, or others, tell God you are willing to be the answer to your own prayers. If your neighbor is lonely and needs a friend, tell God you are willing to be that friend. If your neighbor is in need of some help, tell God you are *available*. If your neighbor needs a word of encouragement, tell God you would be honored to give that kind of message. As followers of Christ, you and I are blessed to be a blessing. Tell God of your availability to be a blessing in your neighbor's life today.

Then—get ready. Whenever a follower of Christ steps up to the line, God begins to open doors of opportunity. Don't miss any of them today!

DAY 4

Alert

"The eyes of the Lord are on the righteous and his ears are attentive to their prayer."

1 Peter 3:12

You may already have noticed that when you make the commitment to pray for your neighbor, the Holy Spirit develops the desire within you to care for your neighbor. When you make yourself available to God, he will take you up on your offer. So, please, for Jesus' sake and your neighbor's sake, be *Alert.* Follow God's example. Keep your eyes and ears open, attentive, and ready to respond.

Relationships with your neighbors can be based on a variety of things. Be alert to how the Spirit may open doors for you to grow in your relationship with your neighbor.

Keep your eyes and ears open, not in an intrusive or nosy way, but in a way that reflects the concern of Jesus for each individual. Look for small and seemingly insignificant ways in which you can serve your neighbors. Don't make a big deal out of the things you do. Your neighbors may not even notice at first, but that doesn't matter. God notices.

For example, when you drag your trash barrel back up the driveway, maybe you could drag your neighbor's barrel up too. If a stray newspaper is caught in your neighbor's shrubbery, pick it up. Also be *alert* to ways in which the Holy Spirit will open up ways for you to engage in conversation and service.

Let me tell you about one of my red-letter experiences. Years ago I lived on the sixth floor of a high-rise apartment building in southeast Denver. My neighbor, Vera, was an elderly woman. During the four years that I was her neighbor, I never observed anyone coming to visit. Her life seemed to center around three outings a day—in the morning, in mid-afternoon, and late in the evening—when she would take a walk with her pet schnauzer, Otto. One day I realized that I had missed Vera and Otto. So I wrote a note that simply said, "I've missed you and Otto. Is everything okay?" and taped it to her apartment door. That evening, when I returned home, there was a note taped to my front door. It read, "I didn't think anyone would notice. Otto is dead."

It didn't take a lot of intelligence for me to realize that my neighbor was suffering from a deflated self-image and grief. I took the elevator back downstairs, walked across the street to the bakery, and bought a half-dozen cookies. I returned to Vera's front door and knocked. "How about making me some tea?" I asked. That night Vera and I shared tea and cookies. We also shared our stories, and she cried softly but deeply as she shared how much she missed Otto.

That conversation helped lead into a friendship between Vera and me. Vera isn't a Christian . . . yet. But throughout the years her Christmas cards have changed from those with little dogs wearing holiday bows to cards with a spiritual hint to them. And Vera keeps asking questions about my church and my relationship with Jesus. The Holy Spirit is working in Vera's life, and I know that someday she's going to take that critical step into her Lord's open arms.

Be *alert* to what's happening with your neighbors. When God opens a door, walk through it.

Reflect/Act

- Spend some time thinking about how much peace you experience knowing that your loving and powerful God is always watching over you and is ready to listen to you.
- Take a walk around your neighborhood. What do you see that tells you something about your neighbors and their needs?

Prayer-Starters for Praying 1 Peter 3:12

Praise God for the amazing truth that he is concerned about even the mundane and insignificant things that happen in our lives. Nothing we bring to him is too small for his attention and concern.

Thank God that he has promised not only to listen but also to be thoughtfully attentive to all your prayers.

Ask God to sharpen your spiritual sight and hearing to the needs and concerns of your neighbor.

Pray a BLESSing on your neighbors:

Be specific today. You've prayed for your neighbors for quite some time, and God has been softening your heart and intensifying your senses to be more and more *alert* to the special concerns that fill your neighbors' lives. What are they?

Body. Pray today that your neighbors may be free of any frustrating illnesses or nagging physical discomforts.

Labor. Pray that your neighbors' employment may provide opportunities for them to express themselves in creative, meaningful ways. Ask your neighbors how their work is going, and ask how you can pray for them in their everyday work.

Emotional. Ask God to help you be *alert* to your neighbors' emotional health.

Social. Pray that God will keep you *alert* to the opportunity simply to be your neighbors' friend.

Spiritual. Pray that you will be *alert* to the questions your neighbor may have about God and about having a relationship with him.

Accepting

"Come, see a man who told me everything I ever did. Could this be the Christ?"

John 4:29

At the center of any good relationship is an *Accepting* spirit. All of us have our funny little tendencies and flaws; all of us have rough edges; all of us have habits that can be irritating.

Your neighbors may not always be the easiest persons to have a relationship with. They may be engaged in habits that offend you. They may have made choices that you would never have made. They may not live with the same values or follow the same rules. They may not discipline their children in a way that you respect. Maybe they play their stereo at ear-breaking volumes. Maybe they use cooking spices that permeate the apartment complex. Or perhaps they are committed to a religious stance that is totally opposed to Jesus Christ. Worse yet, they may be completely hostile and openly judgmental of your life and your commitment to Christ.

Jesus accepts each of us exactly where we are. In his conversation with the woman at Jacob's well in our Scripture for today, he talked with her about her current relationship and her previous marriages. (See John 4:1-30.) He didn't condemn her on the spot. He treated her with respect as a human being. But having done that, Jesus also worked with her to bring her to a better place in life and into a life-changing relationship with him.

God's goal, and our goal with him, is to do whatever is possible to bring our neighbor into a personal relationship with Jesus as Savior and Lord. But, please, as you develop a relationship with your neighbor, do so with an accepting spirit. *Accept* your neighbors as human beings who, like yourself, have funny little tendencies and flaws, some rough edges, and some irritating habits. Beginning your relationship with words of judgment or correction won't enhance the work of the Spirit in their lives or your involvement with them.

Once they come to know Christ, they will join you in submitting themselves to the Holy Spirit's transforming work in their lives. They will begin to become more and more like Jesus as the Spirit works in their hearts, making them pure and holy. Leave that work to the Spirit. Your responsibility is to provide them a safe, accepting, and nonjudgmental relationship. The greatest blessing you can bring into your neighbor's life is the blessing of *acceptance* and love—God's love.

Reflect/Act

- In what ways are you a flawed person?
- Can you think of any judgments you may have passed on your neighbors for things they have done or left undone?
- What can you do to show an accepting spirit to your neighbors today?

Prayer-Starters for Praying John 4:29

Praise God, who is perfect, for his ability to *accept* us in love even "while we were still sinners" (Romans 5:8).

Thank God for accepting you.

Celebrate with God his ability to love the unlovable, accept the unacceptable, and forgive the sinner.

Ask God to help you develop a more *accepting* spirit. *Ask* the Holy Spirit to grow in you the fruit of the Spirit, especially in your relationships with neighbors, classmates, co-workers, and others who may be different from you.

Pray a blessing on your neighbors, using Romans 5:6-11:

Ask God today to help you be the reflection of his *acceptance* and love for your neighbor, knowing that Christ died for each one of us because we are "powerless" to save ourselves.

Ask the Lord to help your neighbors see that "while we were still sinners, Christ died for us."

Pray that the Holy Spirit will work in your neighbors' hearts, even as they are God's enemies, to reconcile them to God "through the death of his Son" and to save them "through his life." Also ask the Spirit to help you love these neighbors, even if they are acting as enemies toward you.

Ask the Lord to move your neighbors to join with you as you "rejoice in God" for the reconciliation (restored relationships) "we have now received" through Jesus Christ.

Pray also for your neighbors' various daily needs, opening yourself to love and *accept* your neighbors with grace and truth.

A FAITH-SHARING METHOD

Using the *Jesus* Video

The *Jesus* video is an 83-minute film depicting the life of Christ. With virtually every word taken from the gospel of Luke, it's the most accurate film ever produced about Jesus. Teams of specialists worked five years filming this video at more than two hundred locations in Israel.

This video teaches about the birth, life, death, and resurrection of the most influential and controversial person in history. It answers questions about who Jesus is, gives insights from his teachings and how they impact people's lives—even today! The video ends by inviting the viewer to pray a prayer of commitment.

The *Jesus* video makes evangelism easy. Many people have become Christians by watching this video and praying the suggested prayer at the end. A recent survey by the Barna research group revealed that, on average, one person prayed the prayer for every two videos given.

How to Use the *Jesus* Video

- Lay a strong foundation of prayer for the people you intend to give the video to.
- View the film yourself, taking note of what it will mean for your neighbors to see it.
- Personally present the video to neighbors and encourage them to watch it. Share the experience you had in watching it.
- Many people give a small gift of food, such as a plate of cookies or a bag of popcorn, along with the video.
- Special seasons, such as Easter or Christmas, are especially good times to consider giving this gift.
- The video can also be left for a neighbor by means of a doorhanger or sent by mail.
- Continue to pray that those who have received the video will watch it and make a commitment after viewing it.
- Make a follow-up call to find out if your neighbors have watched the video and made a commitment.
- Offer a Bible study to those who have made a commitment or have expressed an interest in learning more about God's love for us in Christ.

The *Jesus* video is available from Campus Crusade for Christ. For information and orders, call 1-888-537-8736; e-mail: info@jesusvideo.org; website: www.jesusvideo.org

Determine a Need

Determining a Need

Praise the Lord, O my soul; all my inmost being, praise his holy name. Praise the Lord, O my soul, and forget not all his benefits—who forgives all your sins and heals all your diseases, who redeems your life from the pit and crowns you with love and compassion, who satisfies your desires with good things so that your youth is renewed like the eagle's.

Psalm 103:1-5

When visiting my home last week, my nephew said, "I'm really hungry!" Without too much thought, I knew that he had noticed the empty candy jar in the living room. He wanted some chocolate—his and my favorite.

I wonder how he would have responded if I had offered to get him some broccoli? That wouldn't have fed his "hunger." A hamburger probably wouldn't have done the trick either. Neither would a hot dog.

My nephew was looking for chocolate! His need wasn't really an empty stomach. His parents feed him regularly. No, his need was related to his "sweet tooth"—something I can strongly identify with.

When sharing about Jesus and his gospel message with your neighbor, it's very important for you to be sensitive to your neighbor's individual, specific need. If I had given my nephew some broccoli or a hamburger, I would have missed his real need.

As we learned last week, Jesus comes very intimately, very sensitively into each of our lives. He meets us exactly where we are. He's available to meet each individual need.

As you continue developing a relationship with your neighbor, start asking yourself this question: "What area, what concern, what question in my new friend's life is most in need of the presence of Jesus?"

You don't have to go far to find a possible answer to that question. Answer it for yourself. You have more in common with your neighbor (even your unsaved neighbor) than you might care to admit. Your neighbor most likely has some financial concerns. Don't you? Your neighbor may not be feeling appreciated at work. Have you ever felt that way? One neighbor may be concerned about her youngest child. Another may be concerned about his oldest. Maybe you know what that's like.

Or perhaps your neighbors had a major scare last week when their doctor told them the results of a physical exam. Or maybe your neighbor lost her mother to cancer last fall. You know these things could happen to you, if they haven't already.

Your neighbor's needs are similar in many ways to your own. This week ask the Spirit to help you be sensitive to what those needs are. Look for opportunities to help your neighbor in specific ways. In the next four days we'll look at four needs that you and your neighbor have in common, needs that Jesus addresses in the gospels.

Reflect/Act

- In what ways has God met your specific needs in his surprising, creative ways?
- Don't forget God's benefits. In fact, make a list of them right now. Take note of how the Lord uniquely ministers to your individual needs.
- What things do you hold in common with your neighbor? Are you both too busy? Are you both stressed over finances? Do you have a common concern for your children? Find out by talking with your neighbor this week.

Prayer-Starters for Praying Psalm 103:1-5

Praise God and thank him for all his benefits in your life.

Celebrate God's creativity, thanking him for the way in which he takes into account our unique personalities as he reveals himself to us.

Thank God that he loves all of us enough to meet us right where we are.

Ask God to help you understand your neighbor's unique personality. Invite God to open your mind to the specific way in which your neighbor would be most open to hearing or seeing or experiencing the things of God.

Pray a BLESSing on your neighbors, co-workers, classmates, or others:

Body. Pray that these neighbors may praise God today for his benefits of health, medicine, rest, and relaxation. Ask God to heal all your neighbors' diseases and to renew their strength.

Labor. Ask God to help your neighbors appreciate the skills and abilities they have, and to think about who blessed them with these gifts.

Emotional. Pray that God may satisfy your neighbors' desires and emotional needs, as only he can.

Social. Pray that your neighbors may enjoy the time they spend with friends, family, and anyone else today.

Spiritual. Ask that your neighbors may confess all their sins and experience God's forgiveness, love, and compassion. Pray that they may know for certain that God has taken note of them.

DAY 2
"I'm Too Busy"

"Come to me, all you who are weary and burdened, and I will give you rest. Take my yoke upon you and learn from me, for I am gentle and humble in heart, and you will find rest for your souls."

Matthew 11:28-29

I do not run like a man running aimlessly; I do not fight like a man beating the air.

1 Corinthians 9:26

One need that both you and your neighbor most likely share is relief from the all-encompassing busyness that seems to pervade our culture. Your neighbor has a schedule that is mind-boggling. You know this because your schedule is equally busy. So much busyness can lead to all kinds of fragmented, almost meaningless activity. It can also bring on stress and anxiety.

If you're bothered and frustrated by your busyness, you may need to ask a few questions:

- How do I set priorities?
- What's really important in my life?
- How do I make those hard decisions between working longer hours at work, spending time with my spouse and children, getting the exercise I need, serving in my church and community, and so on?
- How can I learn to say no? To what should I say no?
- How do I slow down this merry-go-round before my life spins out of control?

Each of us, you and your neighbor included, has occasional problems with busyness and the inability to set priorities. When things get out of hand, some very important things usually get pushed to the background. It's almost impossible, we think, to tell our boss that we can't put in the extra hours at work—so it's our spouse or children who often get the short end of the stick.

Watch your neighbor. Maybe he or she shares this problem of busyness with you. If so, you both need relief. Look for opportunities to help each other out with this problem. Maybe you can decide to hold each other accountable for the use of your time. Maybe you can share some of the chores you have in common around your homes. Two working together always makes the job go faster—and often more pleasantly. Here's an illustration you can share with

172

your neighbor: Did you know that an ox, by itself, can pull four to five tons? That's a lot. But two oxen, yoked together and working as a team, can pull up to 22 tons! Amazing!

Here's another thought. Meister Eckhart, a thirteenth-century German theologian and mystic, wrote, "The devil has a device called busyness with which he tries to convince Christians they are really doing the will of God." Have you ever found this to be true?

Share your problem of busyness with your busy neighbor. Who knows how the Spirit will help both of you in living a more balanced and Christlike life?

Reflect/Act

- What would the Lord have you do about your schedule? What should be added? What should be deleted?
- Has Satan, in any way, caused you to confuse your busyness with spirituality?

Prayer-Starters for Praying Matthew 11:28-29 and 1 Corinthians 9:26

Ask God to help you set Christ-honoring priorities in your life.

Thank God that he gives you just the right amount of time to accomplish his will and to give you rest in your life.

Ask God for his help in dealing with any busyness you need to get under control. Tell him also that you're willing to receive your neighbor's help, or that you'll work cooperatively with him or her to solve a shared problem.

Invite God to open your mind to ways in which you can address the problem of busyness with your neighbor in a way that will draw you both to the Scriptures and to what Jesus has to say about this issue in your lives.

Pray a blessing on your neighbors and yourself:

Busyness has hit epidemic proportions. Pray that you and your neighbor may be able to honestly share with each other how this "disease" has affected your lives and how it can mix up your priorities. Pray that God will bless you with the knowledge that he wants you to live at peace and to find your rest in him, not to run some hectic race with the clock.

Where Am I Headed?

"Enter through the narrow gate. For wide is the gate and broad is the road that leads to destruction, and many enter through it. But small is the gate and narrow the road that leads to life, and only a few find it."
Matthew 7:13-14

Another need you share with your neighbor is one that could really help you focus on important issues in both of your lives. Every day we make decisions that reinforce the development of the person we will be in the future. The choices we make today determine what our life will be like down the road. Every one of us needs to take a look at the values we are setting for ourselves.

Some believers and mis-believers alike have chosen to live a life of "me first!" They maneuver to get ahead of anyone else in the checkout lane. They put a spin on the truth in a way that magnifies themselves and enlarges their reputation. That's a path that sets their lives on a certain trajectory.

Some believers and mis-believers have chosen to live a life in which their career is most important. Everything else falls somewhere in line behind the job. That, too, is a path that sets their lives on a certain trajectory. It's usually a path that leaves one's spouse, children, and friends in the dust.

Still other believers and mis-believers look at life as an opportunity to be of service. They open doors for others. They greet friends and strangers with cordiality. The choices these people make on a day-to-day basis set their lives on a trajectory as well.

Which kind of person are you becoming? Which kind of person do you want to become?

This is another issue facing both you and your neighbor. If you've developed a relationship with a neighbor next door or with a co-worker, classmate, or someone else, it's rather easy to discuss this issue. Ask your neighbor what she wants to be. Ask your neighbor whether he thinks he's heading in the direction he wants to go in. Talk about the direction you're going.

Conversations like this provide incredible opportunities to share the reason behind the choices you have made as a follower of Christ.

Reflect/Act

- Evaluate the direction of your life. What things are most important to you? What do you want people to say about the life you have lived?
- Based on your observations, what things are most important to your neighbors? Find out more by getting to know your neighbors better.

Prayer-Starters for Praying Matthew 7:13-14

Talk with God about your goals. Are they God's goals for you, or are they simply yours?

Invite the Holy Spirit to do whatever is necessary to get you pointed in the right direction. Ask God to help you stay focused every day on him.

Ask the Spirit also to give you insight into the direction your neighbor's life is headed. Pray for that neighbor, and ask the Spirit to help you be available as a guide to the way Jesus wants him or her to go.

Pray a BLESSing on your neighbors:

Body. Pray that your neighbors will care for the bodies God has given them and seek to honor him as their Creator and Lord.

Labor. Ask God to help your neighbors find the right place for their work or career in view of his will for their lives.

Emotional. Pray that your neighbors may be at peace on the pathway God calls them to follow, not turning to the right or to the left but finding their full satisfaction in the Lord and his one way to life.

Social. Ask God to shield your neighbors from making poor decisions and taking dangerous turns to please their "friends" or just to follow the crowd.

Spiritual. Pray that all your neighbors will choose the way "that leads to life" and that the Lord will walk with them every day, revealing continual signs of blessing and hope to them.

DAY 4

Who Am I Serving?

"What good is it for a man to gain the whole world, yet forfeit his soul?"

Mark 8:36

I'm convinced that everyone wants to do something significant with his or her life. Really! Do you know of anyone who honestly would say they don't want to make some kind of contribution or leave some kind of impression on this world? No one has a life that doesn't matter. No one is insignificant. In fact, every one of us is far more than significant. Every one of us is made in the image of God!

So it's not strange or even wrong for any of us to hope that when we leave this life, someone or something will be affected. We want to leave some kind of legacy.

That's a need you share with your neighbor.

Both you and your neighbor have a need planted in you by God to live a significant, meaningful, valuable life. God created each of us to fulfill a divinely ordained purpose. He gives us talents and abilities. He gives us a world to live in, a world to care for, a world to enjoy. God asks us to represent him by giving us responsibility for the care of the earth and all its plants and animals. Through the prophet Jeremiah God says that his desire is to give us "hope and a future" (Jeremiah 29:11).

The best way to guarantee that your life has significance, and that it leaves an impression that outlasts your time here on earth, is to commit yourself to some kind of service. Think of the people in history who are the most warmly remembered and highly honored. They're the people who gave of themselves for others in the name of one cause or another. They gave of their time, talents, and energy to do something right or to make an improvement that would benefit people. When we think about such people, we might be reminded of world leaders, brilliant scholars and inventors, brave soldiers, inspiring athletes, great artists, generous millionaires, and more.

The greatest person in all history, however, is the One who gave himself totally and perfectly to the service of God's kingdom. Jesus Christ came willingly and humbly to give up his life and then conquer death so that all people might have life forever. And he calls us to follow his example.

Jesus helps us to focus our service by reminding us that God's will for our lives is to love God more than anything or anyone else, and to love our neighbor as ourselves (Matthew 22:37-39). So if I make the commitment to love God with everything I am, that means I love God with all my heart, soul, mind, and strength for Jesus' sake. And if I love God that way, I also make the commitment to love my neighbor, whom God loves.

This means my life will be rich with right relationships in Christ—with God and with my neighbors. And by God's grace this means my life will have great significance and be secure with God forever!

Reflect/Act

- If I could watch you today, what would I be able to conclude about whom you are serving? What would clearly be most important in your life? Would it be your spouse, the clock, your work, the "bottom line," yourself, or God?
- List three things you can realistically do to "love your neighbor"—anyone who lives or works near you. Make plans to do those things.

Prayer-Starters for Praying Mark 8:36

Invite the Holy Spirit to show you what benefit you are gaining by the way you are living your life. Are you in danger of gaining the world but losing your soul?

Ask God to live in and through you so that your life will leave a God-glorifying impression on the people around you.

Ask God, again, to give you the courage to invite your neighbor (sensitively) into a discussion about the direction and significance of your lives. For starters, here's a question you might talk about sometime: "I wonder what our children will remember about us after we're gone?"

Pray a BLESSing on your neighbors who live or work near you:

Body. Ask God to impress upon your neighbors how significant their bodies are to him as temples of his Holy Spirit.

Labor. Pray that your neighbors will see the significance of their work today—for their families, for others, for their own well-being, and for the Lord.

Emotional. Pray that your neighbors may understand clearly that their lives are significant—indeed, that they are precious to God, who made them in his image.

Social. Ask the Lord to help your neighbors see that their relationships with others are significant and that they are called to love their neighbors as they love themselves, out of love for God.

Spiritual. Pray that your neighbors will also see that their relationship with God is the most important thing in their lives, and that they may live in a way that gives others this impression.

DAY 5

Future Shock

"Do not worry about your life, what you will eat or drink; or about your body, what you will wear. . . . Look at the birds of the air; they do not sow or reap or store away in barns, and yet your heavenly Father feeds them. Are you not much more valuable than they? Who of you by worrying can add a single hour to his life?"

Matthew 6:25-27

As I am writing today, the economy is strong. Interest rates on loans went down earlier this week. The economic future seems bright. But tomorrow everything could change.

Yesterday leaders in the Middle East met with the U.S. Secretary of State and made some progress toward peace. Last night there was a terrorist bombing. Today the U.N. Security Council is meeting again to discuss genocide in the Kosovo province of Yugoslavia. When will the fighting ever cease?

Another thing you share with your neighbor is concern about the future. That means you both need assurance about the concerns you have.

And what are your concerns? Well, your concerns aren't only for national and international things like the economy and world peace. Your concerns are most often centered closer to home. You're concerned about your children's future, perhaps, or about who will care for your aging parents, or about who will care for you. Your concerns on a daily, weekly, and monthly basis are focused on food to eat, schedules to keep, the viability of social security, and how you are going to make next month's mortgage payment.

Your most important concern, though, if you're a Christian, is your relationship with God. All your other concerns pale in comparison to this one. And God is the only One who can take care of all those other concerns.

In our Scripture passage for today, Jesus reminds us of this fact—and more. He states clearly that worrying about any of these concerns is a waste of time and energy, a waste of part of our precious gift of life. And he assures us that since we are "much more valuable" than the birds of the air, whom our heavenly Father feeds faithfully, surely he will take care of all our needs and concerns. This is not to say we don't have valid concerns. But we do have to trust him.

One of your neighbor's needs is to know that the God who created him or her is the God who has promised to walk with us every step of the way through life, caring for our every need. (See Psalm 23:1-4.) Have you ever spoken with

178

your neighbor about that need to know? If not, ask God to help you find a way to speak that word of assurance. God wants that neighbor to know, and he wants you to work alongside him, sharing the message of his great love and care for everyone through Jesus Christ.

Reflect/Act

- What worries you most about the future? What does Jesus say you can do with that worry?
- Are any of your concerns ones that you share with your neighbor? If so, the next time you talk about those concerns together, be ready, at the Spirit's leading, to share God's message of assurance with him or her.
- In what ways, if any, does your neighbor figure into your dreams about the future? Will you be together in God's presence? Why, or why not? Have you done everything you can to help God change that future?

Prayer-Starters for Praying Matthew 6:25-27

Thank God for his promise to walk with us every step of the way through life, assuring us that he will meet all our needs. Tell him you appreciate and value his leadership in your life.

Commit your future to God's care. Entrust to God the lives of the people you know, including family members, co-workers, and neighbors.

Ask God for an opportunity to talk with your neighbor about the future. There are all kinds of topics you can use for starting points: the economy, the political climate, the stock market, the new millennium. Don't miss the opportunity to share the peace and joy you experience knowing that God is in control and that he has a future designed for each one of us.

Pray for your neighbors, using ideas from Psalm 23:1-4:

Ask God to assure your neighbors that he is their Shepherd, so they "shall not be in want."

Pray that they may trust in the Lord to provide food and drink and restoration for their souls.

Ask that the Lord will guide them "in paths of righteousness" so that they may be merciful, just, and humble in all their dealings with others.

Pray that even if they are in "the valley of the shadow of death," they will be comforted, knowing their Shepherd is protecting them and walking with them every step of the way.

A FAITH-SHARING METHOD

Using a Bible Verse— Romans 6:23

Begin with a question. Ask your neighbors if they would like to understand the basic message of the Bible. Tell them it can be summed up in one verse. Ask if they would like to look at and explore that verse with you. If they would, go on.

Turn to Romans 6:23. If you have a Bible with you, invite your neighbors to read Romans 6:23 out loud to you. If you sense that they're not comfortable doing that, read it to them. Write out the verse on a napkin or piece of paper so that you can work with it. (Be sure you have the verse memorized so that you can do this even if you don't have a Bible handy.) Here's the verse:

> The wages of sin is death, but the gift of
> God is eternal life in Christ Jesus our Lord.
>
> Romans 6:23

Explore words and phrases in the verse, boxing each word or phrase as you focus on it. Ask questions about these words to see if your neighbors understand what they mean, and make comments, if necessary, to get at their true meaning. Here are some questions and answers to use with each word:

Wages—What are "wages"? *(What we earn by the work we do. What we deserve to be paid.)* Fairness requires that we be paid what we have earned.

Sin—What do you think of when you hear the word "sin"? *(Sin is missing the mark, not living up to God's standards. A sin could be an action, a thought, an attitude, or even not doing something we should have done. Not loving God, for example, is a sin.)* Do you think I am a sinner? *(In God's eyes I am.)* If this definition of sin is right, do you think God would consider you a sinner?

Death—How would you define "death"? *(Death is the end of life. It also means separation—as in the separation of life from the human body. It also means separation from God.)* If a person is separated from God after dying, what do you suppose that means? *(God is the source of all good. The only thing left without God's presence is the place where there is no good—hell.)* I can't think of anything worse than to be separated from God, the source of all good, for all eternity, can you?

Summarize/Discuss

At this point you can summarize in a way like this: "So these words tell us that, because we have not lived up to God's standards, we deserve death—hell—eternal separation from God. Do you agree that this is what these words say?"

If your neighbors do not agree at this point, you may need to discuss sin, death, and hell with them further. Silently ask for the Spirit's leading in this matter. Try to find out what your neighbors' ideas about these things are. It's likely that they haven't even thought much about them before. Be prepared to tell what the Bible says about these things, explaining passages like Genesis 3; Matthew 13:24-30, 36-43; Luke 19:10; John 3:16; 1 John 1:8-10; 3:8; and Revelation 20:11-15. You may want to mark the passages in your Bible before-hand, in case you need to refer to them. Remember also to mention that the Bible is our only source of truth about these matters. God has given us his Word in the Bible to make us aware of our sin and to show us the way of salvation. (See 2 Timothy 3:14-16.)

Even if your neighbors do not fully agree at this point, invite them to continue talking with you about the rest of Romans 6:23. Before they admit that the Bible is true and that they are sinners in danger of death, your neighbors may need to hear that God has provided a way out. Deep down, your neighbors already know they are sinful (Romans 1:18-25). What they need most is to hear the message of God's grace. Let the gospel message here speak for itself.

But —The word "but" gives us hope and suggests that there may be an alternative to hell. And there is!

Gift—What is a "gift"? *(Something given to show love.)* What's the difference between a gift and wages? *(You don't have to work for a gift or earn it some-how.)* What's the most basic thing you do when offered a gift? *(You accept it.)* How do you feel toward someone who gives you a gift? *(Thankful, loving.)* A gift, by its very nature, cannot be earned. It is given simply because the giver freely chooses to give it.

Eternal life—What do you think "eternal life" is? *(It's a life full of joy and peace that starts on earth and lasts forever. It's a life in relationship with God—as opposed to death, which is separation from God.)* Is that something you would like to have? This verse is telling us that eternal life is available as a gift! Isn't that amazing?

Of God—Do you think of God as a person? *(Though he is invisible and differ-ent from us in many ways, God is a person who thinks, feels, wills, and wants to have a relationship with us.)* Why would God want to give us such a gift? We don't deserve it! *(We really matter to God! We are his sons and daughters. God loves us very much and wants us to be part of his family forever.)* How does that make you feel about God?

181

Jesus Christ—Do you know who Jesus Christ is? *(He is the true Son of God, sent from the Father and yet one with the Father and the Holy Spirit. Jesus became truly human to make it possible for us to have "eternal life.")* Do you know why he died on a cross? *(To receive the "wages" of our sin—that is, to bear the punishment we deserve and to save us from that punishment, which is death.)* Do you know why he arose from the grave? *(To show that he conquered death by purchasing new life for us, through his shed blood.)* It's because of what Christ has done that God offers us the gift of eternal life.

Lord—What do you think it means to be "Lord"? *(It means to be the one in charge, the one who has authority. Jesus now has "all authority in heaven and on earth" [Matthew 28:18]. He rules in heaven with love and righteousness. As you serve him, he will guide your life so well through his Holy Spirit that it will be full of joy and peace.)*

Comprehension Question

At this point, it would be a good idea to ask, "Does this make sense to you? Is there anything about this verse that is unclear?" Clarify if you need to.

Clarifying Comment

Romans 6:23 is a Bible verse that begs for a response. In order to receive the gift of eternal life, it's necessary to respond to God with regard to *sin,* his *gift offer,* and his *authority as the Lord of life.* Everyone needs to . . .

- *admit* being a sinner, who deserves the wages of death.
- *ask* God for forgiveness and for the gift of eternal life.
- *agree* that Christ is the Savior and Lord who has all authority to rule and guide each person's life.

Commitment Question

Ask your neighbors, "Have you ever said these things to God? If not, is there any reason why you can't say them right now?"

Suggested Prayer

Here's a way to lead your neighbors into prayer to God: "A good way to actually start a relationship with God is to pray—that is, to talk to him about these things. Could you, for example, say . . .

"God, I admit that I am a sinner and that I deserve the wages of death—eternal separation from you. I truly want eternal life. I accept your offer to give it to me freely through Jesus Christ. I sincerely thank you for this gift. I willingly trust my life to the rule and guidance of your Son, the Lord Jesus Christ."

Praying the Prayer

Invite your neighbors to make these words their prayer to God. If they truly mean these words, God will respond by giving them the gift of eternal life immediately.

You may want to give your neighbors the option of closing their eyes and repeating the words after you, phrase by phrase. Some may even prefer to verbalize their own prayer that reflects the content of the prayer above. That would be wonderful!

Celebrate

If your neighbors have sincerely prayed such a prayer, rejoice with them over their new life and their new relationship with God. Assure them that something really did happen in their relationship with God, even if they don't "feel" any different. (Explain, if you need to, that salvation is not based on a feeling. It's based solely on God's gift of faith in Jesus, recognizing and honoring him as Savior and Lord.) Encourage your neighbors to continue talking with God and listening to him through his Word, the Bible, so that their relationship with him will grow strong.

Future

Keep the door open to future meetings with these neighbors, if at all possible. They will need your help and/or the help of other Christians to continue to grow.

Direct the Gospel

DAY 1

Directing the Gospel

I have become all things to all men so that by all possible means I might save some.

1 Corinthians 9:22

You'll never hear me criticize the idea of street-corner preaching. But you'll probably never see me preaching on a street corner. I'm grateful for those who are able to preach in places I simply cannot. I don't have the courage. I'm not fast enough on my feet. I might not always appreciate the tactics of street-corner preachers, but I admire their courage and passion.

On a recent visit to Boston I spent a Sunday afternoon in Harvard Square. For about an hour I listened to two street preachers. One stood there until some unsuspecting pedestrian would walk by. With volume that set some people back on their heels, the young man screamed his one-line message at the top of his lungs. "Repent! God finds your sin repulsive!" It didn't matter if the pedestrian was a child or an elderly man, a businesswoman, a beggar, a prostitute, or a student. The message was always the same.

His message spoke the truth. All of us need to repent of the ways we have sinned against God. And God does find our sin repulsive. But I found myself wondering if this young man's message was the most appropriate for each individual crossing his path.

Just down the block I listened to another street preacher. His approach was different. His voice was strong, but not piercing or harsh. He stood in one spot and yelled, "I'm a Christian. I'd like to tell you about what that means. May I try to answer any of your questions?" And on that balmy, spring, Sunday afternoon in Boston, literally dozens of people had questions. Some questions sprang from cynicism. Some were asked in rather abusive ways. One young man, his jaw clenched, said, "My mother died last month of cancer." Then he asked, "How can you even think about the existence of a God who lets something so horrible happen to a woman who never did anything wrong?" But then another man, whom I had seen begging earlier, quietly asked, "How can you be so sure?"

The preacher's answers were thoughtfully put together. To some of the questions, he simply said, "I'm sorry, but I don't know how to answer that." His eye contact with each questioner showed warmth and intensity. He treated everyone, even the hecklers, with respect. I've rarely observed anyone with so much inward and outward control.

To the majority of the questions he responded by telling a story about Jesus from the gospels. This young man tried to listen carefully to understand the particular need of each person in his audience and then proceeded to direct the gospel message to that need.

You and I can learn a lot from that second preacher. Your neighbor has particular needs. The Bible speaks to each one of them. Some of our neighbors need to hear, "Repent! Your sin is repulsive to God!" But others need to hear, "God so loved the world that he gave his one and only Son" (John 3:16). Still others need to hear, "Come to me, all you who are weary and burdened, and I will give you rest" (Matthew 11:28).

Last week we spent time determining the needs we share with our neighbors. This week let's learn new and sensitive ways in which we can direct the message of Christ to the specific needs of our neighbors. Looking at last week's needs, let's use the next four days to look at how you and your neighbor can open the Bible and discover together how the Lord addresses the shared needs in each of your lives.

Reflect/Act

- With whom has God uniquely designed you to communicate? Who would best hear the gospel message from you, rather than from someone else?
- What adjustments are you willing to make to share the gospel with your neighbors?

Prayer-Starters for Praying 1 Corinthians 9:22

Thank God for the person(s) who introduced you to Jesus.

Ask God to lead you to the people he wants you to share his message with. Be courageous. Ask for a list of half a dozen.

Praise God for the providence that brought you to live or work near your neighbors. These are people with whom you can talk about your relationship with Christ.

Tell God you are willing to do anything outside of sinning to share the gospel message with your neighbors, so you can help "save some."

Pray a BLESSing on your neighbors today:

Body. Pray that your neighbors will not distrust God if they are suffering from terrible diseases. Pray also that they may be healed.

Labor. Ask God to speak to your neighbors' hearts today in the midst of their work and to motivate them to work for his glory.

Emotional. Pray that your neighbors may be assured that they are important to God, who created them in his image.

Social. Ask God to bless your neighbors with joy and fun in their relationships with others, and pray that they may praise him for it.

Spiritual. Ask God to do whatever is necessary to bring your neighbors to himself, using you in whatever way he chooses.

"I'm Too Busy" II

"Seek first his kingdom and his righteousness, and all these things will be given to you as well."

Matthew 6:33

I'm writing this in the fall. Where I live, the leaves are falling. Across the street one of my neighbors is trying to stuff them into leaf bags decorated to look like pumpkins. It's not going very well. As soon as she gets a rakeful into the bag, a gust of wind unleashes twice as many leaves onto her lawn. I can tell by the tension on her face that she's not exactly enjoying the autumn season. It reminds me of what we learned a week ago about something we have in common with our neighbors.

Often it feels as if there's so much going on in my life that as soon as I check off one thing (get one leaf in the bag), twice as many more things pile up to be done (the wind unleashes twice as many leaves).

How would you direct the gospel message to that problem you share with your neighbor? How do you think that might work?

Offering to help my neighbor rake the rest of her leaves would give me a great opportunity to share with her what I am thinking before I go out with my rake. I could say something like this: "Cleaning up leaves would be enough. My problem is that there are about as many things on my 'To Do' list as there are leaves in my yard. How about you? I sure am glad God gave me some help in setting some priorities. He even promises to help get things in order when I follow through on his priorities."

You see, God has given us some great insight into our busyness problem. Jesus says in his Sermon on the Mount that if we set our priorities on seeking first the kingdom of God and living in right relationship with him, he'll give us what we need in all the other areas of our lives.

My neighbor might ask, "Sounds great, but how do you do that?" That would be a holy moment. It would give you the opportunity to be honest and transparent enough to share that all kinds of things compete for priority in your life. It would open the door for you to share with your neighbor that your most important challenge in life is to turn to God first for help, to fill your thoughts with his desires, to follow Jesus' example, and to serve and obey him in everything.

If you're not careful, anything can quickly bump God out of first place in your life. But if you keep God front and center, it's a lot easier to fight the busyness battle. You could even go on to ask if your neighbor might be willing to help keep you accountable. What a phenomenal way for you to help each other grow closer to God!

Reflect/Act

- Start practicing. Look out your window. What do you see? Leaves falling? Rain? Snow? Sunshine? Are there any neighbors out there? Rain reminds me of God's faithfulness. The rainbow reminds me of God's promises. Heighten your own personal ability to see God in the things and events that surround you and your neighbor on a daily basis. Find a way to talk to your neighbor or help with a job that needs to be done. Let God's Spirit guide you in what to say.
- What's first in your life? Using the leaf analogy, what would be the first "leaf" you'd put in the bag? Is seeking God's kingdom and living in right relationships with God and others at the top of your list?

Prayer-Starters for Praying Matthew 6:33

Praise God for his kingdom and his willingness to allow the sacrifice of his only Son to bring you into a right relationship with him.

Confess any situations in which you've been so distracted that God hasn't received first place in your day. Ask God to help you place him first.

Ask God to sharpen your knowledge and memory of the Bible. Ask him to remind you throughout the day to reflect biblically on your experiences, on what you see, on what God reveals about himself.

Offer yourself to God by letting him know you'd be honored to use whatever ways he chooses to bring his truth into your conversations and relationships with your neighbors.

Pray this prayer for your neighbors today:

Dear Lord, give my neighbors experiences today that draw their attention to you. As your Spirit works in their lives, help them to be responsive to your leadings. Bless my neighbors through me today in some way. I ask all this for Jesus' sake. Amen.

Where Am I Headed? II

Whatever is true, whatever is noble, whatever is right, whatever is pure, whatever is lovely, whatever is admirable—if anything is excellent or praiseworthy—think about such things.

Philippians 4:8

Every day of your life, you and your neighbor are making decisions that set the direction for your future. Even the little decisions.

The way we spend our time, the directions we take, the way we set priorities—all of these things affect us and the people we live with and make plans with. Even a little decision we make at one point in the day will affect what happens later in the day. Of course, we don't want to get anxious or obsessed about our decision-making. And we can't avoid making decisions! But it's wise to be aware that even little decisions have some sort of effect on our future. And if that's true, think how much our big decisions affect our future!

Where are you and your neighbor headed? What trajectory are you on? Taking into consideration the decisions you have already made today, where are you going to end up?

The Bible is filled with divine wisdom about decisions to make and how to make them. One way for you and your neighbor to set your sights on a direction that God will bless is to take a look at the Ten Commandments. (See Exodus 20:1-17.) Holding each other accountable for loving God, honoring your parents, speaking the truth, and showing other people love and respect are great ways for you to begin sharing the life-giving truths of the Bible.

The book of Proverbs is a great place to gather some great advice too. It's useful for the practical decisions you and your neighbor make every day. Think about inviting your neighbor to join you in reading a chapter a day for a month; that will take you right through the book. Share the insights you gain from this discipline.

One of the most interesting Bible texts is Philippians 4:8, our Scripture for today. It addresses one of the major concerns we have about information and thinking in our society. For example, with access to information and data on the Internet, we have more information than we know how to use, more information than we need to know, and lots of information that is unhelpful and even dangerous to know. Anyone who has "surfed" the World Wide Web has found that our conscious and unconscious decisions online can lead us to places we had no intention of going.

The apostle Paul says, "Whatever is true, whatever is noble, whatever is right, whatever is pure, whatever is lovely, whatever is admirable—if anything is excellent or praiseworthy—think about such things." If your thoughts are in the right place, your decision-making is taking your life in the best possible direction.

Pray for God's guidance in your decision-making. Look to his Word for direction. Invite your neighbor to join you, and make yourselves accountable to each other and to the Lord.

Reflect/Act

- Where are you headed? What criteria do you use in making decisions about the future? Is God's Word the first place you turn to, or the last?
- Do you really believe the Bible contains wisdom for living today? Be honest. Have you checked out some of its advice? Have you ever put it to the test? Try it today.
- Commit yourself to reading a chapter a day from Proverbs. It's great stuff!

Prayer-Starters for Praying Philippians 4:8

Praise God that he is true, noble, right, pure, lovely, admirable, excellent, and praiseworthy.

Confess any wrong turns you may have made lately in your life. *Ask* God to lead you and help you stay pointed in a right direction that honors him.

Invite God to work in your heart in such a way as to increase your excitement about sharing all of his goodness, beauty, power, and majesty with your neighbor.

Pray a blessing on your relationship with your neighbor:

Be confident of the Spirit's working in your neighbor's life. Be aware that the devil may be trying to scramble communications and distract your neighbor's thinking (and yours). Pray that you and your neighbor may listen carefully to the leadings of the Holy Spirit and avoid making poor decisions and heading in wrong directions. Pray that together you will find much in the Bible to guide you and to praise God for.

Who Am I Serving? II

"The most important [commandment] . . . is this: 'Hear, O Israel, the Lord our God, the Lord is one. Love the Lord your God with all your heart and with all your soul and with all your mind and with all your strength.' The second is this: 'Love your neighbor as yourself.' There is no commandment greater than these."

Mark 12:29-31

Me. My. Mine. Sometimes I'm embarrassed with how many times these three words come out of my mouth. We can be such selfish people.

You and your neighbor fall into this category too. Each one of us needs to learn how to balance *Me* and *My* with *You* and *Your.* God created all of us to be in serving community with each other. Our greatest fulfillment comes from loving our neighbor as we expect to be loved ourselves.

But you and your neighbor might also fall into another category. The other side of the coin is that many of us are overcommitted. Our lives are so filled with meeting other people's expectations and schedules and needs that we don't have a moment for ourselves. One of my neighbors would become very wealthy if she made ten dollars every time she ran one of her four children to school, a soccer game, a music lesson, or a scout meeting. You and your neighbor might share her problem. Together it might be helpful for the two of you to spend some time learning together what God would describe as his "best" for you. God provides just enough time each day for us to accomplish his perfect will.

Look for an opportunity to discuss with your neighbor what balance might look like in your life. The Bible tells us that God is number one. But the Bible also teaches us that God wants us to live full and complete lives. Being a doormat for anyone and everyone else in our lives is not what God has planned for us. Serving Christ as number one brings fulfillment and satisfaction. Serving Christ first gives us the stamina and the energy to serve others in his power.

Who are you serving today? Who is your neighbor serving? Could you share some of this over the fence or the coffee table today?

Reflect/Act

- Who is at the center of your life? I've found it helpful to draw a target and write the names of people (including myself) on that target. Is God at the bull's eye? Or is it me pushing to get to the center again? How is it with you?
- Reflect on what your life will look like if you fully love the Lord your God with all your heart, soul, mind, and strength.

Prayer-Starters for Praying Mark 12:29-31

Praise God that he is the center of our lives, whether we recognize it or not.

Ask God to remind you throughout the day of the centrality of his presence in your life.

Ask God for an opportunity today to have a conversation with your neighbor about whom the two of you are serving. Add a request for God to give you courage to have this conversation. I'm finding that I am sometimes more afraid of my neighbor's resistance to such conversations than necessary. And I am pleasantly shocked more and more often at how the Holy Spirit has worked in my neighbor's life long before he leads me into a conversation with him or her.

Thank God that his Holy Spirit has been working ahead of you in your relationship with your mis-believing neighbors.

Pray a blessing on your relationship with your neighbor:

Pray today for God to use you as a loving blessing in your neighbor's life. Just as God loves you, commit yourself to loving your neighbor. From that springboard God's Spirit can do miraculous things. In view of loving your neighbor, use the *BLESS* acronym to pray about your neighbor's specific needs. Also ask God to help you and your neighbor keep the right balance between loving the Lord, loving yourselves, and showing God's love to others. Ask the Spirit to work miracles in your neighbor's heart today and to lead your neighbor to tell you how God has been working in his or her life.

DAY 5

Future Shock II

*"I know the plans I have for you," declares the Lord, "plans to prosper
you and not to harm you, plans to give you hope and a future."*
Jeremiah 29:11

What's next? In some situations, of all the questions we ask in our lives, this
one can cause us the most anxiety.

What were the words that caused you the greatest fear in elementary school?
"Take out a clean piece of paper and a sharp pencil. We're going to have a surprise quiz!" Later in life, it tends to be questions like, Will I get the job or not?
Will I lose my position in the company's next merger? What will the doctor
discover? What will the test results show?

A fear of the future, or at least a bit of uneasiness about it, is something you
share with every one of your neighbors. We all have insecurities about our marriages, our jobs, our health. We all have misgivings about what our children
might spring on us next week. We doubt the future of the stock market. We
question how viable Social Security will be when we reach retirement age.

The future is also a rather "hot" topic these days. Psychic hotlines seem to be
all the rage as slick advertising pops up on our television screens. For the life
of me, I don't understand how folks can be taken in by these scams, but it obviously has a lot to do with how gullible we are to thinking we can get a peek
into the days ahead.

Pick up your concern for the future and face it head-on with your neighbor. No
matter what the psychics tell you, none of us has an inside line. But God does.
The prophet Jeremiah records a profoundly helpful promise that comes right
from the God who knows everything: "I know the plans I have for you . . . plans
to prosper you and not to harm you, plans to give you hope and a future."

God doesn't let us in on the future. He asks us to live one day at a time. What
an exciting element you could add to your relationship with your neighbor if,
together, you could share how God day by day by day reveals his plan for your
lives.

In Christ, it's a good plan. You have a future, and it is filled with hope.

Reflect/Act

- Are you afraid of the future? If so, what frightens you about it? Don't be afraid to ask these questions and to answer them honestly. What you hold in common with your neighbor provides a great beginning to some important discussions. Walking together into a growing and deepening relationship with Christ is a great privilege and honor you can share with your neighbor.
- Has your worry ever solved anything? (See Matthew 6:27.)
- What do you think of the fact that God has a plan for you? Do you have any idea what it might be?

Prayer-Starters for Praying Jeremiah 29:11

Praise God for the love he shows you not only in giving you life but also in custom-designing a plan for you.

Praise God that he has plans for every person he has created.

Ask God to give you deepening insight into his plans for you. Ask God also to give you a sense of what his plans are for your neighbor.

Thank God for his commitment to give you all of his divine resources to insure the fulfillment of his plans for you.

Pray a blessing on your relationship with your neighbor, using 1 Peter 3:15 and ideas from today's reading:

Pray that both you and your neighbor may "set apart Christ as Lord" and trust God with every detail of your future.

Ask that your neighbor may have the incredible gift of knowing God has a plan for his or her life. Pray also that your neighbor may have a glimpse of what that plan might be.

Pray for an exciting opportunity to have a discussion with your neighbor that leads to a commitment to hold each other accountable for fulfilling God's plans in your lives.

Pray that together you may "always be prepared" to tell anyone "the reason for the hope that you have." Pray also that you may "do this with gentleness and respect" to "everyone who asks."

Preparing Your Own Testimony

A testimony is an explanation of what God has done and is doing in your life. The apostle Peter urged believers, "Always be prepared to give an answer to everyone who asks you to give the reason for the hope that you have" (1 Peter 3:15). A good way to be always ready to "give an answer" is to carefully think through and write out your own testimony of how God has saved you and has given you hope.

Hints for Preparing Your Testimony

- Begin by asking God to remind you of what he has done in your life and to guide you in sorting it all out.
- Exalt Jesus Christ in your testimony. It's an acknowledgment of the miracle Christ has done in saving you. Give him the credit.
- Use common, everyday language. Avoid religious words unfamiliar to most people.
- Start with a brief introduction, then divide your testimony into three parts: before I came to Christ, how I came to Christ, and after I came to Christ.
- Keep it short enough so that it can be shared in three to five minutes.

Use the following format for your testimony and look through the statements to stimulate your thinking. Focus on the statements that speak most clearly to you.

Introduction
Start with a brief statement of what Christ's love means to you personally.

My Life Before I Came to Christ
Think through and/or write about things like . . .
- what your life was like before you met Christ.
- who or what the major influences were in your life.
- what sin-problems you were experiencing.
- what made you aware of your need for Christ.
- what brought you to the point where you turned to Christ.

How I Came to Christ

Think through and/or write about things like . . .

- what caused you to believe you could trust God—insights or ideas that helped move you in the right direction.
- how you came to know Jesus Christ in a personal way.
- what you sensed Christ had done for you.
- what gave you assurance of eternal life.
- Scripture passages that spoke to you.

After I Came to Christ

Think through and/or write about things like . . .

- the most striking change in your life.
- what your relationship with God is like now.
- the blessings you now experience as a child of God.
- the areas you are still working on.

Ending

State clearly what your listeners need to do in order for God to work in a similar way in their lives. They need to . . .

Admit that they have sinned and need to be forgiven.

Believe that Christ died for them to remove the guilt of their sin and give them eternal life.

Commit to love and serve God the rest of their lives.

Keeping on Track

DAY 1

Keep On Track

I pray that you may be active in sharing your faith . . . .

Philemon 6

Develop a relationship, determine a need, and direct the good news of Jesus to that need. If you commit yourself to these three things in relation to your neighbor, you will be at the center of God's plans to use you in extraordinary ways in your neighbor's life.

Commit yourself to following the Spirit's leading as you move through these three stages. Be honest about which stage causes you the greatest uneasiness.

I'll be honest. Sometimes my pride gets so much in the way that my fear of failure keeps me stuck somewhere between stages two and three. And that means my efforts fall short, because having a relationship and determining a need doesn't introduce someone to Christ and his saving message. The good news (gospel) must be shared and heard, spoken and received.

During this final week of *Developing a Prayer-Care-Share Lifestyle* we're going to take a look at some things we have to do if we're going to live so that the Holy Spirit can use us in sharing the gospel with our neighbors. I personally cannot think of any other experience in the Christian life that is more humbling or exciting than to have the Spirit use me—even in a small way—to bring another person closer to Christ. If you have never had that experience, "beg" God for that gift. In the next few days I want to share with you some experiences I've had in which God simply did miracles in a relationship with someone.

One of the important ways to "keep on track" is to make sure you have a plan. Don't let a day pass by in which you aren't daily praying for a friend, a neighbor, a co-worker, a family member, or someone else who hasn't yet turned his or her life over to Christ. Make the commitment to jot down, at least once a year, a list of the people in your relational circle who haven't yet turned their lives over to Christ. If you haven't done this, do it today, and then set an easily remembered date—such as your birthday, Christmas, Easter, or January 1—to review your list and to add to it. Write the names down and keep them in a place where they will catch your eye regularly. Then make sure you pray every day for the people on your list.

Don't let today pass without asking God to bring to mind the names of two or three people you can pray for, care for, and share Jesus Christ with. List their names here:

1.
2.
3.

If you can't come up with three, that's okay. Ask God to bring one or two more people into your life.

Reflect/Act

- What is easiest for you—developing a relationship, determining a need, or directing the gospel to meet that need? Celebrate the gifts God has given. Ask for his help in any area that may frighten or intimidate you.
- At what point in this process does Satan tend to trip you up?

Prayer-Starters for Praying Philemon 6

Praise God for his willingness to use us, of all people, in his enterprise to save those who are lost!

Thank God for his promise to give us everything we need in order to communicate our faith and the message of Christ's good news.

Thank God that his Holy Spirit has been working in our neighbors' lives through a variety of other people and experiences even before we have met them.

Ask God to keep you active in sharing your faith.

Pray a BLESSing on your neighbors today, as you include specific items you are aware of:

Body. Ask the Lord to strengthen your neighbors and give them energy and good health today.

Labor. Ask that your neighbors' work today will be focused, productive, and filled with satisfaction from a job well done.

Emotional. Pray that the peace and joy of the Lord will reign in your neighbors' lives today, causing them to give thanks to him.

Social. As your neighbors interact with others today, pray that God's love may shine *to* them *through* others (including yourself) and *through* them *to* others.

Spiritual. Ask God to draw your neighbors closer to himself today, pouring out his Spirit on them. Pray also that God will use you as he wishes to work in your neighbor's life today, whether it's through praying, caring, or sharing his message of love—or all three!

DAY 2

Be Interruptible

I heard the voice of the Lord saying, "Whom shall I send? And who will go for us?"
And I said, "Here am I. Send me!"
He said, "Go . . . ."

Isaiah 6:8-9

Of all the household chores, I hate ironing the most. I hate it so much that I have my shirts laundered.

April (not her real name) works early mornings at the cleaners. We're on a first-name basis. She knows I'm a pastor. I know she is single and cares for three elementary-school-age grandchildren. While it has been rather obvious to me that April likes to talk, she hasn't shared with me whether she's divorced or widowed, and I don't know the circumstances that led her to take in her grandchildren. Several months ago she asked if she could "confess" to me that she hadn't been to church since she was married, except for a handful of funeral services and an occasional Christmas and Easter service.

You need to know that last January 1, I put April on my "hit" list. I've been praying that God would use me in any way possible to share Christ with April.

Recently I stopped at the cleaners on my way to an early-morning meeting. I was running late, but I thought that if I could just run in and out, I could make my meeting on time. It looked possible. There were no other cars in the parking lot. April was at the computer when I came in, so she immediately typed in my name, noting the four shirts I brought in and the "on hangers and heavy starch" instructions. As I was reaching for the door, I said, "Have a good day!"

April responded with a sober, "I will, physically."

I'm not the most sensitive person in the world, but even I recognized her words as a rather unique response. Within a fraction of a second the Holy Spirit reminded me that one stressed-out grandmother is of infinitely more value to God than any meeting. The Spirit sensitized me to the fact that I just might be on the threshold of an interruption that could turn into a holy moment. I decided to be obedient to the Spirit. I asked, "April, is there something wrong with the rest of you?"

With tears welling up in her eyes, April told me that she didn't think she could keep up with the pace of caring for her grandchildren. She just felt overwhelmed and alone. With a choking voice she asked, "Do you think God would be willing to come back into my life?"

Within the next two to three minutes I had the profound honor of being able to lead April in a prayer of recommitment to the Savior and Lord she had left decades earlier.

God loves to interrupt our lives—not in a negative way but in a way that surprises us with opportunities to join him in his mission here on earth. God's will is always done, regardless of our responsiveness. But don't miss the excitement of being interrupted from what you have planned. God wants you to join with him in fulfilling his plan.

Reflect/Act

- Have you ever told God that he may interrupt you? God's plan will be accomplished through someone, but he isn't in the habit of drafting someone into service. He uses volunteers.
- If God wanted to "send" you somewhere to someone, could he find room in your schedule?

Prayer-Starters for Praying Isaiah 6:8-9

Praise the Lord for his great plan of salvation and for his willingness to use us to help bring others to him.

Confess any carelessness you may have shown by not listening to others' needs for spiritual comfort or for not being available to share Christ with others.

Ask God to give you the willingness to be used by him. Like Isaiah, pray this prayer: "Here am I. Send me!"

Ask God for the courage to be obedient when he takes you up on your offer.

Pray for your neighbors as your relationship with them develops:

Ask God to help you pray faithfully for the people on your prayer list. Review the BLESS prayer in connection with your neighbors. Continue to be more specific in your requests as your relationships with them grow. Pray also that if God chooses to "send" you to your neighbors, you will be willing and interruptible. Ask for God's help in setting priorities so that you can be available. Ask for wisdom to speak God's message of love and salvation in a way that meets your neighbors' needs.

DAY 3

Know Your Context

Buy the truth and do not sell it; get wisdom, discipline and understanding.

Proverbs 23:23

I will never grow tired of watching the Holy Spirit at work. He uses such unique and curious ways to bring people to a relationship with Christ. That's why it's so important for us to commit to being able to use every opportunity to be witnesses for Jesus' sake.

The second thing we have to do is commit ourselves to know the context we are working in. Make yourself available to conversations with your neighbors about a whole variety of subjects. Most of your neighbors will need to be comfortable in talking with you about common, everyday things before they'll be comfortable in talking about their spirituality. Don't ignore what might be important or interesting to your neighbor.

How can you be ready to talk about a variety of subjects? Be aware of what's happening in the international political scene. Know which movies are drawing the crowds in your hometown. Know the titles on the best-seller book lists. If your neighbor has a dog, do you know what breed it is? If your neighbor gardens, have you asked to take a closer look? Do you know which schools or colleges your neighbor's children attend? Ask about their holiday traditions. Ask about their unique professional challenges. Ask about their favorite foods.

The Holy Spirit can use any one of these topics as an entrance point for you to begin a conversation that can help you develop a relationship with your neighbor. And as you develop a relationship, you'll begin to know your neighbor's heart, and your neighbor will begin to know yours.

Let me tell you about one such experience. Several years ago I was privileged to be part of a new church-planting ministry. Early in that project the members of the core group went door to door, interviewing neighbors to find out the needs of the families in the area around our new building site. We expected that one point of contact would be time management or the setting of priorities. We anticipated holding Christian perspective seminars on those important topics and inviting our unchurched or mis-believing neighbors as our guests.

But do you know what the number-one need in our new and fast-growing neighborhood turned out to be? Potty training!! That's right. These upwardly mobile, extremely busy, work-addicted "busters" perceived that their number one "crisis" was in knowing how best to help their young children (and there were thousands in that community) outgrow their need for diapers. So we responded by hosting a "Potty Training" seminar, to which we invited a pediatrician, a child psychologist, and our neighbors.

And do you know what? As a result of the relationships that gradually developed between church members and the one hundred neighbors who met at that three-hour seminar, ten persons eventually came to know Jesus as the Lord of their lives.

Know your neighbors. Know what's important to them. Be able to have intelligent conversations with them about the things they value. As followers of Christ, we need to "earn" the right to speak to the most important, eternal needs of our neighbors. Start to earn that right by knowing the context of their everyday lives.

Reflect/Act

- How have your prayers increased your desire to know your neighbors in a caring way?
- What have you learned about your neighbors? Commit to learning more and more about them so that you can relate to them in a way that shows God's love for them and leads to sharing the good news of Christ.

Prayer-Starters for Praying Proverbs 23:23

Praise God for being the most intelligent, brilliant being in the universe! Our God knows everything!

Thank God for his offer to give us wisdom when we ask for it (James 1:5).

Ask God to "wise you up" regarding what's going on in our world. Do that for two reasons—so you can pray in a more informed way, and so you can increase the possible "connections" between you and your neighbors.

Pray a blessing for your neighbors, using ideas from 1 Corinthians 2:6-16:

Pray that the Holy Spirit will protect your neighbors from the "wisdom of this age" so that they may understand "God's secret wisdom" revealed by his Spirit.

Pray that your neighbors, with all the data available to them in this "information age," will not be distracted from the message of "what God has prepared for those who love him"—that is, life and peace in the Lord's presence forever, through Jesus Christ.

Ask the Holy Spirit, who "searches all things," to help you understand what your neighbors' needs are.

Pray that your neighbors, in the context of so much spiritual searching in our culture, may find Jesus Christ as the one, true way to the Father.

Pray that both you and your neighbors may "have the mind of Christ."

DAY 4

Know Your Bible

Blessed is the man . . . [whose] delight is in the law of the Lord,
and on his law he meditates day and night.

Psalm 1:1-2

The song "Thy Word" is one I sing often. Not out loud. My singing voice is best used only in private worship. The words go like this: "Thy Word is a lamp unto my feet and a light unto my path." These words are based on Psalm 119:105. These words from the Bible are true not only for my personal walk with God but also for my walk in praying, caring for, and sharing with my neighbors.

You will never be able to direct the gospel to your neighbors' unique needs unless you know the Bible. Keep reading and learning from the Bible. As you read and think about a certain passage of Scripture, begin by asking the Holy Spirit to apply the Word and its truth to your life. Also be courageous enough to ask, "Does this part of God's revelation include anything that addresses a need in my neighbor's life?"

Let me share another story with you. During a hot, humid day in August, I walked out onto my deck at the back of our house. My neighbor was watering some of her potted flowers on her deck. She had not had a great summer. Her allergies had been causing some real discomfort, a relative had died, and her struggle with depression was starting to feel like a losing battle. After I greeted her that late afternoon, she sighed, and said, "I suppose the Bible doesn't address people with my concerns, does it? Christians are supposed to be happy."

Obviously my neighbor wasn't asking me to affirm her misguided notion about the psychological happiness or sadness of believers in Christ. What helped her that day was that the Holy Spirit reminded me of the words of a psalm I had read earlier that week—Psalm 69. I said, "Wait just a minute. I'll be right back." I grabbed my Bible from inside the house and was able to read the opening lines of Psalm 69:

Save me, O God, for the waters have come up to my neck.
I sink in the miry depths, where there is no foothold.
I have come into the deep waters; the floods engulf me.
I am worn out calling for help; my throat is parched.   (vv. 1-3)

I think you can well imagine the conversation we were able to have, and the open door the Lord gave me that day to talk with my neighbor about his sensitivity and concern toward her.

She responded by saying, "God does understand me. Maybe no one else does, but he certainly understands." Standing together on our adjoining decks, we read through about a dozen other psalms. The Bible seems to cover every human emotion. From the Word of God, my neighbor received permission to feel her depression and to share it with God. Then his Spirit gave her insight on how to handle it for that day.

Know your Bible. It's a big, thick book, but don't let that scare you. It's God's Word of love, understanding, and salvation for our sake. It's our one reliable guide for living. If you don't know much in the Bible, read something new today. But keep learning more. Ask for the Spirit's guidance to understand what you read, and study it with other Christians who can help you understand it.

God knows what he's doing. God has put his power into the words of Scripture. And he promises, "My word that goes out from my mouth . . . will not return to me empty" (Isaiah 55:11). God's Word tells us of his love and draws us to him.

The more personal experience you have with God's Word, the more usable you will be in God's great plan for this world and for your neighbors.

Reflect/Act

- Are you a man or woman of the Word?
- What can you do in your life to get to know God's Word better? Do you need to rearrange priorities to spend more time with the Bible? Do you need to join a Bible study? Ask for the Spirit's guidance in this.
- Ask God to help you apply yourself to learning more about his Word so that you can share it with your neighbors and bring God's message of love and grace to them in their various needs.

Prayer-Starters for Praying Psalm 1:1-2

Praise God for giving us his Word, which brings life and joy and shows that he loves and cares for us.

Ask God to lead you by his Holy Spirit to delight in his Word and to learn from it every day.

Ask God to make you a man or woman of the Word and to use you in bringing his Word to others.

Pray a BLESSing on your neighbors today:

Along with the specific BLESSings you ask for your neighbors today, pray that God gives both you and your neighbors the desire to dig deeper and deeper into the Scriptures.

Pray for an opportunity to share God's Word with your neighbors soon.

DAY 5

Keep on Praying and Caring

"All authority in heaven and on earth has been given to me. Therefore go and make disciples of all nations, baptizing them in the name of the Father and of the Son and of the Holy Spirit, and teaching them to obey everything I have commanded you. And surely I am with you always, to the very end of the age."

Matthew 28:18-20

As you finish this set of devotional readings, please remind yourself of two foundational truths: you have to keep on praying, and you have to keep on caring. Otherwise God won't be able to use you to keep on sharing. Without praying and caring, your sharing will be ineffective and will sound only like so many words.

The first important thing you can do for your neighbor is pray. Only in a vulnerable, honest, consistent relationship with God will you be able to follow the Spirit's leading in the next move you can make in your neighbor's life. Some of us have a tendency to rush into a relationship too fast. Others of us are far too restrained and silent to develop relationships in which people feel they can be open and vulnerable. Only in prayer will God provide you with the leading from the Spirit that you will need to know you are moving along in his power.

Be sure, too, always to ask for the Spirit's gifts. He promises to give you the words to speak. He's already been working in your neighbor's heart. The Spirit has brought other people and other experiences into your neighbor's life. The one certain way to guarantee that you are the most usable communicator of God's Word to your neighbor is that you are consistently, daily connecting with God in prayer. And, remember, Jesus himself promises to be "with you always"!

The second important thing you can do for your neighbor is to keep on caring. Care for your neighbor in a sensitive, consistent way. Be aware of how much privacy your neighbor needs. Be aware of how your assertiveness may affect him or her. Be as Christ in his or her life. Your attitude, your kindness, your faithfulness as a friend can speak volumes.

And if you need a role model, look to Christ. He loves you and your neighbor and our entire world so much that he left heaven and became one of us. As one of us, he perfectly obeyed the Father, becoming the perfect sacrifice for our sins. That's how much Christ cares!

In the early days of the church, believers in Christ were known for the way they always prayed for and loved each other. It's a poignant witness to the love of Christ. (See John 13:34-35.) It's the way God calls us to live so that his good news in Jesus can take root in people's lives and keep spreading to "all nations."

Reflect/Act

- What will it take for praying, caring, and sharing to become a permanent lifestyle for you? Think back on all the things we've talked about in this book. Commit to making this lifestyle your lifestyle, for Jesus' sake. Ask for the Spirit's help; he wants to work miracles in you and through you.

Prayer-Starters for Praying Matthew 28:18-20

Ask God to help you bear in mind the essential task of the church and of every Christ-follower. We are called to be witnesses to the gospel of our Lord!

Thank God for inviting *you* to join him in his work in this world.

Ask God to use you and to *continue* to use you in praying for your neighbors, caring for them, and sharing the good news of Christ's love with them, for Jesus' sake.

Ask God for the salvation of your neighbor—and the next one, and the next one!

Keep praying God's blessings for your neighbors:

It cannot be said enough. If you and I, as children of the heavenly Father, keep asking for his Holy Spirit's work in the lives of our mis-believing friends, family members, co-workers, classmates, and others, what will happen to the kingdom of our great God? It will grow!

Pray for "every good and perfect gift" from God, who "chose to give us birth through the word of truth" (James 1:17-18). God's desire is the salvation of the world—and that includes your neighbors.

Pray for God's blessings on your neighbors—it's something you can be sure God wants—along with having you work alongside him in his great plan of salvation.